ADVENTURES OF THE HORSE DOCTOR'S HUSBAND 3

ADVENTURES OF THE HORSE DOCTOR'S HUSBAND 3

JUSTIN B. LONG

Adventures of the Horse Doctor's Husband 3

This is a work of creative nonfiction. The events are portrayed to the best of Justin B. Long's memory. While all the stories in this book are true, some names and identifying details have been changed to protect the privacy of the people and animals involved.

Written by Justin B. Long

www.JBoydLong.com

Published in the United States by Springhill Media, a division of Mad Goat Press

Gainesville, Florida, USA

https://SpringhillEquine.com

Cover Design by: My Custom Book Cover

Limits of Liability and Disclaimer Warranty:

The author shall not be liable for your misuse of this material. This book is strictly for entertainment purposes.

First edition printing September 2023

ISBN 978-1-948169-93-6 (Ebook Edition)

ISBN 978-1-948169-94-3 (Paperback Edition)

ISBN 978-1-948169-95-0 (Hardcover Edition)

Library of Congress Control Number: 2023913414

For Erica, who inspires me to be the best I can be.

Nonfiction Books by Justin B. Long

Adventures of the Horse Doctor's Husband

More Adventures of the Horse Doctor's Husband

Adventures of the Horse Doctor's Husband 3

How To Become an Equine Veterinarian
(co-authored with Erica Lacher, DVM)

The Righteous Rage of a Ten-Year-Old Boy: A Journey of Self-Discovery

Fiction books written under the pseudonym J. Boyd Long

THE DIMWORLD SERIES

Genesis Dimension

When Good Plans Go Bad

Inside The Machine

Table of Contents

Introduction

If you're reading this, there's a good chance you've read the first two books in this series. And if you've read the first two books in the series, there's a good chance you've been waiting a while for Book 3 to arrive. If that's the case, I apologize for the long delay.

As you probably know by now, I'm a big proponent of self-discovery and personal growth. One of the reasons this book took so long to happen is I wrote another book called *The Righteous Rage of a Ten-Year-Old Boy*. It's all about my journey through therapy as I looked back at the abuses and traumas I experienced as a child, and how those events shaped my understanding of who I am. I had to write that book, because I discovered that nearly everything I believed about myself was wrong, and my therapist helped me reframe my perspective on myself, both my child self and my current self. That profound shift in mindset changed everything about my life, and I needed to share that with others. So, if you (or someone you love) struggle with insecurities and self-confidence, you might find it worthwhile to read. Don't worry; the topic is heavy, but the book is very positive. It's still me writing, after all!

If you're new to this book series, I'll catch you up quick. My name is Justin B. Long, and I'm married to Dr. Erica Lacher, who is now probably one of the most famous equine veterinarians in the world. Part of that is due to these books, part to our vet clinic's YouTube channel, and part is due to our podcast, *Straight from the Horse Doctor's Mouth.* At this writing, we're on our sixth season, and the show has become way bigger than we ever could have anticipated. We have thousands of listeners in the U.S., but I never dreamed we'd also be popular in Canada, Australia, and across Europe and Africa.

I met Dr. Lacher in June of 2014. We were both 38, which seemed much older then than it does now. I wasn't a horse person, although I lived on a huge cattle ranch in Wyoming when I was in high school, so I thought I knew some stuff about horses. I quickly realized how wrong I was about that! We married in October of 2015, in a spectacular costume wedding. Erica was Lara Croft, Tomb Raider, and rappelled out of a huge live oak tree in our back yard to the makeshift altar. Her best friend and maid of honor was a banana spider, and also rappelled out of the tree. I was King Arthur from Monty Python's *Search for the Holy Grail*, and my best friend Kristen was my best man. She dressed as a Jedi knight, and clapped the coconut shells for me as I trotted down the aisle on my invisible horse. As you might imagine, it was a lot of fun!

Erica had her own vet practice, Springhill Equine Veterinary Clinic, which she bought back in 2008. When I came on board in 2015, it was a two-doctor practice with a total staff of five people. While I had a variety of skills that applied to managing a business, I had an immense amount of stuff to learn. Somehow, I've managed to avoid bankrupting us, and we've grown to a four-doctor practice with a staff of twelve over the last seven years. While I've done a decent job of growing into my role, I'm still amazed that Erica ever trusted me to run her business, especially considering my knowledge base in 2015 compared to now. I guess she has a good eye for undeveloped potential, and a much higher risk tolerance than I have, as I would never be able to trust someone [me] with our business the way she did!

Erica is one in a million, and I don't just say that because I'm her adoring husband. Most people who have an interaction with her end up feeling the same way. Vet students who mentor under her, staff, clients, podcast listeners, YouTube viewers, other veterinarians, you name it. We all agree that she is the rock star that we aspire to emulate. She has unshakeable confidence, charisma, grace under pressure, and teaches everyone around her in a way that makes them feel like they're on equal ground with her. It's rare to find someone who is so confident and accomplished, yet maintains a healthy level of humility, and us humans are drawn to that. People tell me all the time how lucky I am to be married to such an amazing woman, and I wholeheartedly agree! I'm the luckiest man in the world.

I've talked to a lot of people about horses and books since I started writing this series. There are some recurring themes among the experiences that readers have that I didn't expect, but I've come to understand a bit better. The most prevailing of these that people tell me about is a horse they had thirty or forty years ago, and the feelings they have for that horse are just as strong today as they were back then. I think this phenomenon is what makes horse people unique. We've all had dogs and cats that we loved dearly, and even other humans, but no connection on earth seems to match that of a person and the horse they bond with. That's something I've never experienced, and I'm guessing most people outside the horse world never will.

That's what this book series is about. Having horses is an unbelievable emotional, financial, psychological, and spiritual rollercoaster. Horses will test your capacity for stress and compassion, they'll find obscure ways to severely injure themselves, and they'll make you question your sanity. But they also teach you who you are, and help you become a better version of yourself. They show you how much you can grow, and how much you can love. And they force you to keep your feet on the ground. In the mud. And the poop. And when you have that perfect ride, in whatever way that is for you, it's a high like no other. You can't get that package anywhere else.

This is the third book in this series. It might be a little different from the first two books, because in the world of equine emergency medicine, there are only so many things that happen. The vast majority of the emergencies we see after hours are eye ulcers, lacerations, and colics. I didn't want this book to be repetitive, so I decided to broaden the horizon a bit. While there will still be lots of crazy emergencies in here, we'll also experience some of the other adventures I'm having in this wild lifestyle, and with some of the other doctors in our practice. So, enough intro stuff. Let's start this thing!

1

Hey Mom, Watch Me Jump!

Now and then I get tasked with picking up a horse and taking it somewhere. Sometimes I haul a horse from our clinic to a referral hospital for surgery or an MRI. Other times I pick it up wherever it lives and bring it to the clinic. We'd purchased a brand-new truck recently, so I jumped on any excuse to drive it. You know how it is when you get a new toy.

I had just finished unhooking the horse trailer one morning and was about to pull out of the gate on my weekly feed store run when a text came through on my phone.

Are you able to pick up a mare and foal in Lake City and bring them to the clinic today?

It was Dr. Russel, one of our veterinarians at Springhill. They never asked me to haul a horse unless it was really important, and there was no other way to get it done, so I knew it needed to happen. Lake City was an hour away, and a round trip was definitely going to put a hole in my day, but I sent a quick reply and backed around to reconnect the horse trailer.

I've been pulling trailers a long time, and I know better than to assume that our rig will fit in someone's yard just because they have a horse. We've got more than a few clients that have driveways that could never accommodate a four-horse trailer, and some that couldn't even handle a two-horse. You might be able to pull in, but there's no place to turn around, and backing out onto a road can be a terrifying proposition, even with good backing skills. So, I always take a look at the address on Google Maps if I haven't been there before. I like being prepared.

Dr. Russel sent me the address, and I ran upstairs and looked it up on the computer. The house was off the road in a field, with tons of room to turn around. Perfect! We have a smaller horse trailer that I use when the big one won't fit, but I much prefer the big one. It's a smoother ride for the horse, it has its own brakes, so it stops better than the small one, and as a gooseneck it just pulls better. Since I would be hauling a foal, all that stuff was doubly important.

With the big trailer hooked back up, I started down the driveway once more. I'm a creature of habit and routine, and I've been accused of being OCD, so adapting to this lifestyle was a challenge for me in the beginning. Over time, though, I'd learned to embrace the unpredictable direction changes that wrecked my plans for the day, as they were usually way more exciting than what I'd had planned. This particular mission didn't seem like it would be very thrilling, but it didn't stay mundane for long.

Upon arriving in Lake City, I realized my first mistake, which I'd made an hour before. While I looked at the house and yard on the map, I didn't pay much attention to the roads leading into it. I knew about where I was supposed to be, but not exactly. This was a problem, because the GPS was telling me one thing, and the street sign in front of me said something else. I tend to trust the street signs in these situations. That was mistake number two, but I stand by my logic. The street signs had never been wrong for me before, while the GPS had been wrong plenty of times. Well, there's a first time for everything, right?

I was sitting at the stop sign at a T-intersection. Technically it was a cross, not a T, but the road directly across from me was clearly a private drive rather than a road. It was very skinny, gravel, and the street sign said *Clark Ave.* I was looking for Willow Drive. The GPS was telling me to go straight and I would be at my destination, but I was afraid to trust it. There were blooming crepe myrtles overhanging the narrow single-lane track, obscuring my view past the house on the corner, and the area I could see left me no place to turn around.

There was another road just up from Clark, too far away to read the sign, but close enough that it might be throwing off the GPS. I decided that must be it, so I turned left. I stayed on the left side of the road so I could make the next turn to the right, but I knew right away that this wasn't my destination. The street sign said it wasn't, and the small trailer park behind it backed up that conclusion. I decided to pull in anyway, since it looked like the road looped around the back of the park. I needed a place to stop and regroup, and this was as good as any spot I was likely to find.

It turned out that the road did *not* loop around. I ended up backing the trailer into someone's back yard, praying that it didn't fall through the lid of a septic tank. That happened to me once back when I delivered propane, and one time in a septic tank is enough for one lifetime, I promise. A low-hanging power line forced me to maneuver back and forth a few times to scoot the back of the trailer over while dodging a swing set, but I managed to get turned around without catastrophe, and without getting shot at, which is not always a guarantee in rural Florida.

I parked at the stop sign and pulled the map up on my phone. It showed Willow being the next road down from me, directly across from the intersection. I followed it back on the map, and sure enough, the house I recognized from earlier was in the back. That meant I really, really should have gone straight across when I had the opportunity. Now I was going to have to make a very tight turn onto a very narrow drive with a deep ditch on all sides. I could feel the tension growing in my shoulders.

It's hard to say this without sounding like I'm bragging, but I'm really good at pulling a trailer. I always have been. If I could have picked the thing I have a natural knack for, I probably would have picked something else, like playing the guitar, but trailering forward and backward is what I got. It's useful, don't get me wrong, and on days like today, it was exceptionally useful, and I was grateful for it. But even with my confidence in my skills, I was nervous. This was a bad situation.

The main road was too narrow for me to swing wide,

and the ditches on both sides were deep. The road I needed to turn on was very narrow, with a narrow culvert. There was no room for the trailer to swing. To make matters worse, the street sign with the wrong name on it was near the pavement, making it even narrower. There were also a few trashcans sitting there, which I could see from the next road down. The main road wasn't terribly busy, but there was a car every few seconds, which complicated things.

In retrospect, I should have taken the five-mile backtrack to get back to that intersection on the opposite side where I started again, so I could just pull straight across. Deciding against that plan was a mistake I would lament about a hundred times over the next ten minutes, but I decided to try to make the impossible turn. Why? I didn't want to spend the extra time doing the right thing. I rushed it. I acted on impulse instead of doing the logical thing. Every once in a while, I have to re-learn my lesson on this. Never cut corners (pun fully intended)!

When it was clear, I pulled out onto the highway and turned to the left. I dropped the passenger tires off the pavement, trying to get the trailer as far over to the right as physically possible. I purposefully went past the turn a bit, then backed up with the wheel cranked to the right, jackknifing the trailer. A car pulled up behind me and stopped. He could see what I was doing, so I ignored him and focused on making the turn.

Again, I was in a hurry, so I didn't stop to move the trashcans. Instead, I let the bumper push them over, praying that they weren't full, and that they wouldn't end up tipping over into the ditch. They were on the right, so I lost sight of them quickly as I crept forward. Once the truck was across the culvert, I angled to the right a bit more. However, when I looked in the left mirror a second later, I knew this wasn't going to work. The trailer was still at a forty-five-degree angle, stretched across both lanes, and if I went forward another five feet, I was going to hit the street sign with the side of the trailer. There was just no way to get down this road from the north side.

I was already beating myself up, letting the stress creep in. I put the truck in reverse, knowing that backing out was going to be really dangerous. I had a pretty good chance of either putting the trailer in the ditch on the far side of the road, or dropping the front right wheel of the truck into the ditch. What I didn't expect, as I started creeping back, was for the car behind me to whip around the trailer, passing me half in the ditch. I slammed on the brakes, my heart pounding. I couldn't see to my right due to the crepe myrtle, so I just had to hope that no one in that direction was going to try the same move. I started rolling back again.

Because I had done a two-point turn to get into the road, getting out was even harder than it normally would have been. I had almost zero swing room to maneuver the truck, so I had to pull up and to the left a couple of times to get enough room to get the truck back onto the pavement without falling off the culvert on the right side. This was the part that made me grateful for understanding the geometry and physics involved in micro-positioning the vehicle to get the desired result. Traffic was piling up, but I was able to ignore the pressure and get myself safely extracted from the driveway.

My new problem was that I was back on the main road in an unfamiliar area, heading away from my destination. I needed to find a place to pull over and make a new plan. The GPS in the truck showed a subdivision approaching, and the road was a loop. That would work. I carefully turned off the road, pulled around the neighborhood, and stopped in front of an empty lot. I took a series of deep breaths to calm down and drank some water before consulting the map again.

It took me ten minutes of driving backroads to get back to the intersection where I started out, facing the right direction. I couldn't help but think about the fact that had I taken the time to go around and reset to begin with, I probably would have already made it to my destination, loaded the horses, and been back on the road.

When there was a break in traffic, I eased across the intersection, noting the two trashcans in the ditch. At least there wasn't any trash spilled out; they appeared to be empty. I pushed through the crepe myrtles, making a mental note to stop and rescue the trash cans on my way out, and emerged in a pasture. The dirt road continued down the side of it, and eventually turned to the right, pointing me to the house.

As I drew near, a woman came around the side and waved me to the back. A small, recently-built barn, which was really just two stalls with a roof and a tack room, stood near the trees, and I pulled around in a circle until the side ramp was lined up with the stall door. It was a really neat setup, both visually pleasing and well-designed for the purpose of keeping horses happy. While the stalls were open slats with great airflow in all directions, the tack room was painted a nice teal and decorated with old-fashioned gas station signs and rusting saw blades.

The only information I had gotten from Dr. Russel was an address, a phone number, and the single sentence asking me to pick up a mare and a foal. I hadn't even considered why they might be headed to the clinic, other than to assume that the foal wasn't feeling well or something to that effect.

"Hi, how's it going?" I called out as I ducked under the gooseneck and began to drop the ramp. "I'm Justin, from Springhill Equine."

"Hi, I'm Debbie." She stepped over and shook my hand as I finished opening the trailer. A trim blonde in her early thirties, she looked like she would be more at home in a bank or an office than a barn, but I guess horse people don't always look like horse people. "Thanks for coming to get them. We bought a trailer last weekend, but it hasn't been delivered yet."

"That's bad timing," I laughed, following her over to the stall door where a bay Thoroughbred mare stood with a chestnut foal. "What's going on with your crew?"

Debbie was clearly under the impression that I knew all about her situation as she opened the stall door. "Storm's hematoma split open this morning, and I'm scared to death of doing something wrong that'll end up with him dying."

I don't know if it was the unexpectedness of what was waiting for me that caused my outburst, or the fact that I was already stressed out from trying to get there. The stall door rolled back to reveal a young foal, maybe eight weeks old, with a white blaze and white stockings on both front legs. To my shock and horror, the skin on his chest was wide open. I don't mean there was a slice across it, I mean there was a gaping hole in the shape of a triangle that was literally the size of his entire chest. I could see all the muscles in his shoulders, and inside his chest cavity, all moving as he moved, wet tissue glinting back sparkles of light. I was completely incapable of stopping the words from falling out of my mouth.

"Oh My God! Holy... Wow! I wasn't ready for that. Is he, is that, oh, oh..." At last, the sputtering trailed off, and I realized how wildly unprofessional that had been. "I'm sorry, that was completely uncalled for. I didn't know what I was coming to get, obviously." I chuckled nervously, trying to hide my embarrassment.

"Oh, I said a lot worse than that when I saw it this morning," Debbie said. "Dr. Russel said it's not near as bad as it looks, but it looks pretty bad to me. She told me last week this would probably happen, but I didn't realize it would be so dramatic."

I couldn't help but agree. It looked really bad to me, but I've seen enough to know that you can't judge the severity of something by the shock factor. If Dr. Russel wasn't panicking about it, then I shouldn't either. Still, it looked like his insides could just come spilling out the front, and I had to fight off the images in my head of opening the trailer door at the clinic to find his intestines all over the floor.

"You did a number on yourself, kid," I said, scratching his nose. "What did you do?"

"He tried to jump a fence post about ten days ago and didn't make it." Debbie pointed to the brand-new no-climb fence around the paddock. "We've only had the horses a few weeks. I haven't had a horse since I was a teenager, but now that we got a place out in the country, I've been wanting to raise a foal. I was out here when he did it, because I'd just finished brushing him off and picking up his feet to get him used to it. He ran across there, bucked a few times, then jumped up and landed on the fence post. It didn't break the skin or anything, but it swelled up like a balloon. Dr. Russel's been out here a couple of times, and she told me this morning I could treat him at home, but I'm too afraid. He looks like he ought to be dead any second, and I couldn't live with myself if something happened. I'm glad you can take him to your hospital."

I had recovered my senses by this point. "Well, I don't blame you a bit on that. Let's get a halter on mom. I'll put her in the trailer, and Storm ought to follow her right in there. You might have to steer him a bit. What's mom's name?"

"Sky."

I smiled. Themed names always tickle me. "Alright, Sky. Let's get you on the trailer." I led her out the door and to the base of the ramp, and paused while Debbie and Storm caught up. "I'm going to put her in the front stall, and we'll let Storm run loose in there. Babies travel a lot better when they can get to mom, and the chest bars in here are too high to do much with them, anyway. He may have a problem with the ramp, so be ready in case he freaks out."

She nodded. "Okay, I'm ready."

Sky walked right up the ramp and backed into the front left stall. I patted her on the neck as I latched the chest bar, grateful that she had loaded easy. It doesn't always go like that. She let out a whinny as I removed the lead rope and stepped back, and I just got out of the way as Storm leaped halfway up the ramp like a deer, then jumped inside with a second bound. He obviously didn't like the ramp, but he knew he had to listen to his mom. I hustled out and closed it up before he could change his mind.

The ride back to the clinic was slow and uneventful. Hauling foals requires a lot of concentration, as you have to be very gentle with slowing down and turning. Storm had been on a trailer once before, so he had a head start on getting his sea legs, but I didn't want to risk injuring him in any way, so we took it nice and easy. Dr. Russel had been pretty confident in his condition, so I didn't *really* expect to see anything bad when I opened the trailer door at the clinic, but I wasn't taking any chances.

"Special delivery!" I popped my head in the door at the clinic. "I might need some help steering the foal, if anyone wants to corral a baby with a gaping chest wound."

"Ooh, I wanna see!" Cassie jumped up from the computer. "Is this the one with the giant hematoma?"

"That's the one," Dr. Russel said with a laugh. "We went to see it this morning after it opened up, and Debbie talked us into bringing it here. To be fair, it's a lot to deal with in your first month of horse ownership."

"First month? And she's raising a foal?" Cassie's eyebrows shot up. "Wow, talk about jumping into the deep end of the pool!"

"Go big or go home," I said. "The foal is just testing her commitment, helping her make sure this is what she wants to do."

"Right," Dr. Russel said. "But it's too late to change her mind now, she's committed!"

Everyone in the clinic came out to help unload and see Storm. Sarah had already bedded a stall for them, complete with hay net and water buckets, so all we had to do was get them in it. The trailer ramp was only twenty feet from the barn door, so we didn't have far to go.

"The baby is standing loose," I said as I unfastened the ramp. "I doubt that he'll come flying out, but you never know."

"We got him," Desi said. "After what, four babies born

at the clinic this spring already, I think we qualify as professional foal wranglers."

The other techs laughed in agreement. When we have a mare at the clinic to foal out, they spend a lot of the day out in a paddock, and the nights inside a stall. Moving new foals back and forth every day will build your wrangling skills in a hurry. Unlike grown horses, who have been trained to follow you when you put a lead rope on them, foals can't be led. Or pushed. Or steered. Or coaxed. They will generally follow their mom, more or less, but they get distracted a lot, and it's rather like trying to steer a two-hundred-pound pinball except that they don't follow any laws of geometry or logic. It's something of a sport around here in the spring.

I lowered the ramp to a chorus of assorted sounds of excitement and shock. I knew what they were experiencing, at least the ones who hadn't seen him yet. The cuteness of a foal, with his disproportionately long legs and bright eyes, combined with the visceral experience of seeing his entire chest cavity wide open, brought forth a lot of conflicting emotions. When you're being simultaneously assaulted with cuteness aggression, sympathy, shock, horror, curiosity, sadness, and the overwhelming urge to hug him, it's hard to function for a minute. Fortunately, Dr. Russel and Desi had already been through this experience at the farm and were able to take charge while the others were processing.

"I've got the mare," Desi said, grabbing the lead rope and leaning across Storm to clip it to Sky's halter. "Look out, kid. When I drop this chest bar, your mom might run over you."

Desi pushed Storm to the side with her hip and led his mom down the ramp. The rest of the team formed a lane from the ramp to the stall. Storm stood at the top of the ramp for a moment, watching his mom walk away. He let out a cute high-pitched whinny and reared up, distraught that she was leaving him behind. I stepped up on the ramp with the intention of getting behind him in the trailer, but before I could take a second step, he left the same way he went in: in the air. He landed at the bottom of the ramp in the awkward way that foals have, and raced to catch up to his mom, whinnying and shaking his head. The whole team cheered for him.

Sky and Storm stayed with us for several weeks. The split skin sloughed off after a few days, so he had to grow all new skin on his chest. It took a long time for it to grow in and cover everything, but it finally got there. The daily cleanings and wound care got Storm very accustomed to the halter and lead rope, along with the daily trek to the paddock and back. By the time he went home, he knew all the moves, and probably felt like a grown-up horse. The hospital life isn't the cheapest way to teach a foal to lead and stand, but it's very effective!

2

Bad Mom, Good Baby

I was at the clinic doing some paperwork in the back office when Dr. Lambert, another one of our veterinarians, stuck her head through the door.

"Are you able to help us out for a few minutes?"

"Of course!" I put a paperclip on the page I was on and set the pile aside. "What's going on?"

She glanced behind her to make sure the client hadn't come inside. "We've got to run plasma on a foal, and the mare is extremely aggressive. She tried to kick me twice at their farm this morning when we did the new foal exam."

My enthusiasm waned a bit at that news. "Sounds great."

"Yeah. She's in the front slot on their trailer, so I was

thinking she can just stay there and we'll run plasma on the foal on the trailer instead of bringing them in a stall. We just need a third set of hands to manage the foal."

I followed her outside. The trailer was an old three-horse slant load with equal amounts of rust and faded white paint. I could hear the mare pawing the floor as soon as we stepped out the door.

"The owner is going to try to keep the mare distracted by feeding her bits of alfalfa while we do this," Dr. Lambert said. Her strawberry blond ponytail bobbed as she speed-walked across the grass. "We've got to get a catheter in the foal, so I'll sedate her, place the catheter, and then we'll get the plasma running. It should take about a half hour."

When we rounded the back of the trailer, the mare snorted a few times, looking at us over the top of the divider with a wild eye as she danced around in the slot. A small woman with short, dark hair was standing on the running board, shoving a handful of alfalfa through the open slats on the side of the trailer, but the mare was ignoring her. Cassie stood inside the back end, holding the foal. It was cute as it could be, a dark bay filly with three white stockings and a big blaze on her face. Unlike its mother, the foal was displaying little enthusiasm. She stood there quietly, head drooping. Since it needed plasma, I wasn't surprised at the lethargy. Plasma for a brand-new foal meant it didn't get enough milk on the first day.

Cassie restrained the foal, which is a little different than restraining a grown horse. She slid one arm under the chin and up the other side of its head and grabbed the ear. With her free hand, she grabbed the tail and held it straight up. This kept the foal relatively in place while holding the head up and steady so the vet could get a needle in the jugular.

The foal tried to wiggle at first, but Cassie was ready for it. She used her elbow to raise the filly's chin, and Dr. Lambert quickly found the vein and gave the sedative. I took the empty needle from her, and we waited a minute for the drugs to kick in.

"You just want me to lay her down right here in the trailer, right?" Cassie asked.

Dr. Lambert nodded. "Yeah, that way the mare can see her. Hopefully that will keep her happy."

Cassie maintained a loose hold on the foal as it began weaving. Her head dropped, chin resting on Cassie's arm, and after a few minutes of fighting it, her legs buckled. Cassie carefully lowered her to the floor, and Dr. Lambert helped her get the foal on its side. I grabbed the clippers from the tray outside and passed them to Cassie, then set about getting the rest of the supplies ready to hand to them as needed.

Once Cassie had clipped a square on the filly's neck, I swapped the clippers for the scrub tub so she could clean the area. Catheter infection is just as big of a risk for horses as it is for people, and even though this catheter wasn't going to be in very long, we still wanted to sterilize the area as much as possible. Cassie alternated between gauze soaked in chlorhexidine scrub and gauze soaked with alcohol, cleaning and rinsing, back and forth.

While that was happening, Dr. Lambert was donning sterile gloves. It's an interesting process to watch. The outside of the gloves are sterile, so that means you can't touch them with your bare hands. The cuff is folded over so that you can grab that part and work your hand in, but it's a snug fit, and difficult to do without touching the rest of the glove.

Putting the second glove on has the opposite challenge, as you can't touch the *inside* of it with your sterile glove. The next time you put on a pair of rubber gloves, try to do it as if they were sterile, just for fun!

When they were ready, I handed Dr. Lambert the catheter. Cassie sat down and put the foal's head in her lap to get it above the heart, which would make the IV run faster, and draped a small towel over her eyes. Dr. Lambert uncased the catheter and began palpating the neck, trying to locate the vein. Normally when you clamp down on the general area, the jugular pops up and is easy to find. Since the foal hadn't been nursing appropriately, it was dehydrated, and the vein was almost non-existent.

We were all intently focused on watching Dr. Lambert as she inserted the catheter and gently probed around, trying to find the sweet spot, when the mare kicked the side of the trailer and let out a deafening whinny. I nearly jumped out of my skin. Dr. Lambert never even twitched, keeping the long needle steady. Had I been the one trying to get the catheter in, I probably would have jammed it all the way through her neck in that moment. Fortunately for everyone, I was just holding the supplies tray.

"Hush, now, eat your hay," the owner said, trying to get the mare's focus back. The trailer was rocking with her as she shifted side to side, but it only lasted for a minute. She tossed her head one more time, then went back to eating the hay. I could see the whites of her eye all the way around though, and I knew it was probably a temporary peace.

Dr. Lambert pulled the catheter back out and tried a different spot. I've watched Erica put a thousand catheters in, so I knew there would be a flash of blood up the clear portion in the center when she hit the vein. I also knew that it's really hard to hit the vein on donkeys, minis, and dehydrated foals. I wanted to say something encouraging to Dr. Lambert, but I couldn't think of anything that would do something other than draw attention to the fact that she was struggling.

After a few minutes, she leaned back. "Let's flip her over and try the other side. I don't want to turn her into a pin cushion."

I leaned past her and grabbed the back legs, and Cassie and I carefully rolled her over. "You used up all your good luck on the sedation," I said, straightening the towel underneath the filly. "This is the price for making that look so easy!"

"Yeah, I guess so. I gave that on this side, so maybe it'll be easier."

I handed Cassie the clippers, and she quickly clipped and scrubbed another square. I cleaned up all the dirty gauze as she tossed it out, and soon we were ready to try again.

"Let's get a new catheter," Dr. Lambert said, handing me the old one. "This one's been out too long."

I grabbed a new one out of the tray and passed it to her. Just as it touched her hand, the mare kicked the back wall again, and we both jumped. We laughed, which helped ease some of the tension from the stressful process. Once the mare calmed down, she started the process again.

Five more minutes went by as she probed for the vein. I was about to ask if there was a Plan B when she finally hit it. The vein was deep in the neck, and Dr. Lambert was exceedingly cautious as she eased the needle out and slid the catheter in all the way. When she was satisfied that it was in properly, I passed her the drip set tubing. Once she connected it, I spiked the bag of plasma on the other end and opened the valve.

"Ready?" I asked.

She nodded, and I rolled the thumb wheel. The dark yellow plasma filled the clear tubing, racing down to disappear into the foal. I squeezed the bag to keep pressure on it, trying to get it in as quick as possible. The sedation would only last so long on the foal, and we didn't want to administer a bump dose if we could avoid it.

All went well for the first ten minutes. The mare whinnied a few times, but the foal didn't move. I switched the bag back and forth between my hands. Despite my regular exercise routine, my forearms were screaming from the effort of maintaining a squeeze on the bag for that long.

"I should have been using one of those hand grip spring things that bodybuilders use," I said with a chuckle. "I've determined that my hands and forearms aren't really in shape for this."

Cassie laughed. "I have the same problem. Squeezing the bag uses muscles that you apparently don't use for anything else."

Without warning, the mare reared up, slamming her head into the roof and striking the wall in front of her repeatedly with her front feet while whinnying at a near-scream. When she dropped back down, she began slamming herself around into the walls, kicking and slinging her head from side to side. The trailer was shaking violently, and the noise was deafening. Dr. Lambert pointed outside, and Cassie nodded her head. Together, they lifted the foal and rushed out of the trailer. I scrambled backwards in front of them, trying to keep the IV line off the ground, but not letting it have any tension on it, either. We moved away from the trailer and settled the foal on the ground under a tree. Cassie raced back over and shut the trailer door.

The mare continued to beat the trailer to death for another minute or so. I was sure she was going to kill herself in the process, either from blunt force trauma from rearing into the roof, or from kicking a hole in the trailer wall and ripping her leg apart. It was a testament to the sturdiness of the trailer that it was still in one piece at the end of her rampage. By the time she calmed down, everyone at the clinic was over where we were, clients and staff alike.

"What in the world was that about?" Erica asked.

The owner shrugged. "She's a little feisty, I guess."

Cassie, Dr. Lambert, and I all exchanged a glance. "I think *feral* is probably a better word to describe her," Dr. Lambert muttered.

"I didn't realize you were coming out at first," I said, as the adrenaline rush began to wear off. "I was looking at the horse, and then all of a sudden you were coming at me. That was intense! I'm glad I didn't fall over a tree root."

"We would have run right over you," Cassie said. "I was pretty sure the murder mare was coming out right behind us."

Dr. Lambert chuckled. "It was too noisy to say anything, but I didn't want to stay in there another second. That thing's already tried to kill me once today."

"Sounds like a great candidate for reproduction," I said sarcastically. "Why are we breeding it, again?"

"I know, right?" Cassie rolled her eyes. "But apparently they didn't know she was pregnant when they bought her."

"Wait, they just got this horse?" I tried to wrap my head

around the news. "As in, they found an untouchable horse that wants to kill everyone, and they decided they had to have it?"

"I guess it's a good barrel horse," Cassie said. "I wouldn't have a murder mare, no matter how good it is at its job, but that's just me."

"I'm with you," I said. "Not worth it. It's just a matter of time before you get hurt or killed."

The crowd around the trailer dissipated as everyone went back to what they were doing. I had briefly forgotten about my aching hands, but now that things were settling down, it became my focus again. The bag of plasma was nearly empty though, and I rolled it down to the fluid level.

The foal tried to raise its head, and Cassie peeked under the towel over its eyes. "She's starting to wake up, do you want me to give her anything?"

"Nah, we're almost there," Dr. Lambert said, glancing over at the bag in my hands. "Just make sure she doesn't stand up yet."

Cassie placed a hand on the foal's head. "I've got her. But squeeze harder, Justin." She winked at me.

"I can't feel my hands anymore, but I think I'm squeezing." I held the bag up. "It's almost empty."

When the last drop was down the tube, Dr. Lambert removed the catheter. I cleaned up all the stuff and walked back over to the trailer. The owner was back to feeding the mare handfuls of alfalfa.

"Were you able to get a look at her?" I asked. "It seems like she ought to be pretty banged up after all that."

She nodded. "Dr. Lacher looked at her with a flashlight. She said she's got a small cut on her head, but otherwise she looks okay. I guess there wasn't enough room for her to do too much damage to herself."

"She got lucky," I said. "I'm glad the divider held."

"Me, too!" She let out a laugh that turned into a cough. "This crazy horse can't afford to get hurt too badly, nobody can touch her to fix her up except me. Maybe she'll learn a lesson after this headache."

I doubted it, but I didn't say so. The more likely thing would be that this horse would never receive any of the basics of healthcare, like vaccines and dental care, or even regular trims from the farrier. The best thing that could happen would be the owner doing a ton of groundwork instead of racing barrels, and teaching her to trust people and become manageable. It was possible, but few people were willing to put in the time and effort it would take. That wasn't unreasonable, as we all have busy lives, but it was still sad for the mare.

Once the foal was wide awake, I helped Cassie lift her onto the trailer. The mare nickered at her, and the filly whinnied in her little high-pitched voice in return. I smiled as I closed the trailer door. For all the stress involved in this event, there was still the joy of hearing a foal whinny, and that's something that always makes me smile.

3

The Cost of Stubbornness: A Tragic Tale of Pride and Loss

I'm angry as I write this, so incredibly angry. I'll come back and edit out the swearing, but know that it was here, because I don't have strong enough words for my rage without them.

When I was young, I was always drawn more to Mr. Spock than Captain Kirk. I liked the idea of logic, and always making rational decisions. Human beings aren't like that a lot of the time, and for a wide variety of reasons. I understand that, I really do, but sometimes that lack of logic has a significant impact on others, and that's where I really struggle.

This particular situation started with a phone call, as most of them do, at least on our end. The person on the phone wasn't a client, as they lived well outside of our practice range, but there are no veterinarians where they live, and they had a colic. I happened to be in the clinic when the call came in, and I couldn't help but overhear our receptionist talking to them on the phone.

"How long has she been acting colicky?" Mary asked, her fingers flying across the keyboard as she took notes.

The answer is one that we hear once in a while, but we shouldn't. Ever.

"The horse has been colicking for four days?"

There are generally two reasons that people let their horse colic for four days before calling the vet. The first is ignorance, and I can find my way to forgiveness on that one if I work at it. Everyone is a first-time horse owner at some point, and when you're new, you have a lot to learn. It still seems to me that most people would err on the side of caution if their new horse was acting weird, and I guess most people probably do, but sometimes they don't.

The second reason people wait days to call the vet is money. They're hoping the problem will resolve itself and they can avoid spending $500. This is where logic goes out the window for me. On Day 1 of a colic, it can probably be resolved for $500 and one or two treatments. Not all of them, of course, but most. On Day 2, it's much harder to resolve, and it's probably going to have to be hospitalized and put on fluids, and it might not have a happy ending. Each day you wait past that is going to cost more money to treat, and is less likely to have a good outcome for the horse.

That's exactly what happened here. This person was a horse trainer, so ignorance was not even a remotely believable excuse. No, he wanted to avoid spending $500 on the horse, and in the end, he spent $5,000 and the horse died. That's what makes me so angry my fingers shake on the keys as I type. The horse died, and it died for no good reason. It didn't need to die. It was sixteen years old, and if the trainer, a horse professional who makes his living off this and other horses, had done what a responsible horse owner does and called the vet on Day 1, the horse might have lived another sixteen years. Instead, the horse died, the helpless victim of a stupid human being. Now you know the ending of this story. Here's how it happened.

[Author's note: Juan, the man who is the antagonist in this story, did a lot of swearing. Since I'm trying to keep this book appropriate for all ages while still representing the dynamic of the situation, I used the word "flower" in place of his swear words.]

A woman arrived at the clinic around one that afternoon with the horse. She was young, maybe thirty, and beautiful, with long dark hair. She was distressed, but most people are when their horse is in trouble. As the horse backed off the trailer, I did a double take.

"Why is her mane shaved off?" I asked Erica in a whisper.

"She's a polo horse. That's what polo trainers do."

I shook my head, unable to look away from the strip of skin that ran from her head to her withers. "It's weird. She looks like a moose." Her ears hung out limply to the sides, which added to the moose-like appearance. It was also a sign that she was feeling pretty rough.

Erica's technician took the lead rope from the woman. "I'm Cassie, Dr. Lacher's technician. You're Debra, right?"

The woman nodded.

"We're just going to get her in the stocks and then we'll

check her out. What's her name?"

"Flecha."

"That's right," Cassie said. "Come on in, you can stay with her while we check her out."

They got Flecha in the stocks, and Erica began the exam.

"Temp is one hundred point three."

Cassie nodded as she wrote it down.

"Heart rate is eighty."

"Respiration is thirty."

"No gut sounds."

Erica drew a cc of blood and handed it to me. As a veteran of after-hours colics, I know how to run a lactate test, which makes me feel useful, even though I'm not much of a technician. I grabbed the meter from the counter and inserted a test strip. Lactate meters are just like a glucose meter, but they check the blood for lactate instead of sugar.

"One point three," I announced.

Erica glanced at me. "One point three?"

"That's right."

"Huh. With a heart rate of eighty, I thought it would be higher than that."

Cassie rolled the ultrasound cart over to the stocks. Erica spent the next few minutes running the probe over various places on the horse's abdomen, frowning and muttering to herself. I'd watched her ultrasound a thousand horses by then, and while I couldn't decipher much, I did know how to spot a distended small intestine. I watched carefully, but the small intestine walls didn't look very thick to me. Not thick is good, just to be clear.

"I've got a fluid mass in the abdomen," Erica said. "Not

sure what that is. Could be cecum, or maybe large intestine. Let's see what I can feel on the inside."

Next, Erica grabbed a palpation sleeve and the bottle of lube. Cassie moved up to hold the horse's lead rope while Erica performed a rectal palpation. This part is where she sticks her arm inside the horse to feel what was going on deeper inside than the ultrasound probe can see. After a minute, she pulled her arm out, removed the sleeve, and walked over to Debra, who was watching nervously from the front.

"Well, we've got a pretty sick horse. Her heart rate and breathing are really high, and that means she's in a lot of pain. I gave her some drugs to help take the edge off. I didn't find anything specific I can point to in the gut, and her lactate is normal, so I don't know exactly what's going on. Since she's made it four days, that rules out a few things. The things that it doesn't rule out are all pretty serious. I'd like to do an abdominal tap and run some blood tests, and get her started on IV fluids to work on rehydrating her while we try to get a diagnosis."

Debra shifted her feet, looking down. "How much is that going to cost?"

"She's going to need to be here for a few days, minimum. Fluids are expensive, so I'd say ballpark is $2,500, depending on what we figure out."

Debra pulled her phone out of her pocket with a shaking hand. "I have to call my husband."

She turned away and murmured into the phone. The response was in Spanish, but the enraged shouting coming through the phone was enough to make all of our heads turn. Her shoulders sagged, and as the barrage of fury continued to pour out of the phone, I realized that I had completely misread the situation.

"Dr. Lacher, Juan doesn't want to spend the money on her," she said, turning to Erica. Silent tears were leaking from the corners of her eyes. "Is there something low-cost I can do on the farm for her?"

Erica shook her head. "Can I talk to him?"

Debra said something in Spanish to her husband, then handed the phone to Erica.

"Hi Juan, this is Dr. Lacher. I was just explaining to your wife that Flecha is in trouble, and we need to do something for her, or she's not going to make it."

"I'm not wasting my flower money on this." His accent was thick, but I was able to make out what he was saying. "It's just a flower horse. She can die here for free."

Erica's jaw set, and I knew she was angry, but her voice was as calm as it could be. "I can't send the horse home in this condition. She needs to be treated, or else we need to euthanize her."

"You can't tell me what to do with my flower horse, you flowery flower," he shouted. "That's my flower horse, and my flower money!"

I took a step forward without even knowing what I was doing, and Erica shot me a warning glance. Stepping back, I tried to uncurl my fists. I didn't even remember getting angry, but there I was.

"It's not humane to turn her out in a field and wait for her to die," Erica said. I knew she had to be seething inside as much as me for her to be so direct. "How much would you sell her for?"

"What?"

"How much would you sell Flecha for?" Erica pressed him. "Would you sell her for $2,500?"

"Flower, no, she's worth ten times that," he said. "Are you trying to lowball me because she's sick? I make $2,500 on her in two months of flower lessons. No flower woman is going to steal from me like that. Put my flower wife back on the phone."

"That's exactly my point," Erica said. "It's worth $2,500 to try and save her. Give me a chance to work on her and see what we can do."

Juan was silent for a moment.

"Fine," he snarled at last. "But no more than $2,500. Put my flower wife back on the phone. Now."

Erica's moment of triumph was short-lived, as the verbal barrage poured out of the phone again. I don't speak Spanish, but I recognized a few of the derogatory curse words that men use against women. Debra glanced at Erica, then turned away, her face flaming. She whispered a few more things into the phone before hanging up.

"I'm sorry," Debra said.

Erica gave her a level look. "Debra, this is a safe place for you. If you want help getting out of that situation, we'll find you a place to go."

Debra shook her head violently. "Oh, no, I can't do that. He's not really like this; you're just seeing him at his worst."

"Well, the offer stands."

"Things are different in Argentina," Debra said weakly. "He just doesn't understand how it is here."

Erica turned back to the horse. "Cassie, let's go ahead and get ready to do an ab tap. I want to check the lactate on her abdominal fluid. Let's pull some blood too, and we can run a CBC and chem."

At some point, it occurred to me that Erica was calmly returning to work, while I was debating about jumping in my truck and driving to Juan's farm so I could punch him in the nose a few dozen times. Her professionalism reminded me to use the tools I'd gained through therapy, so I took a few deep breaths. My heart was pounding, but I tried to talk myself back off the ledge. Erica didn't need me to protect her, or defend her honor, and especially not with my fists. If I went and beat him up, he would still be a narrow-minded jerk, and I would be in jail, and Erica would be mad at me for being immature. Being violent wasn't going to teach him a lesson or make him change his ways. If anything, it would just make him worse. After all, his actions were based on insecurities, and that's something I knew all about. My pulse was slowing, but the adrenaline still saturated my blood. Even after rationalizing the situation, it took a few minutes for my hands to stop shaking.

With the decision to try and save Flecha made, Debra went home. It was obvious that she was the one who was trying to care for the horses, while her husband saw them as tools to make money with and to be thrown away when broken. She had to know she was going home to a fight, considering everything that had happened so far. I felt bad for her.

I helped Cassie hang the fluids bags. Each bag held five liters, so they were heavy and awkward to get on the hook at head level by yourself. Once the bags were up, Cassie went to help Erica with the abdominal tap, and I set about getting the tubing connected and ready. It seems like a simple task, but it isn't. The directions have fifteen steps, which is about ten steps too many, in my not-so-humble opinion. We use four bags of fluids at a time, so the drip set has to connect all four bags to a single line that will attach to a catheter in the horse's neck. Despite my grumbling about the directions, I was glad to have them. It took me a while, since I don't do it all the time, but I got it done.

"How's it going over here?" I asked as I stepped out of the stall.

Erica shook her head. "The lactate on the abdominal fluid is normal. Her bloodwork is basically normal. Her heart rate and respiration say she needs to go to surgery, or else be euthanized, but nothing else is backing that up. I don't know what's wrong with her. Maybe it's a slow onset colitis or something. That fluid mass in her cecum could be diarrhea, so we'll watch for that. Otherwise, I think we manage her pain, and try to get her hydrated and see what happens. Dehydration masks things sometimes."

It was a waiting game, so I decided to go home and get some work done. In my world, there is always bookkeeping to be done, a podcast waiting to be edited, a video project waiting to be finished, a book to write, and a long list of farm chores with my name on it. Staring at the horse wasn't going to help the horse.

A few hours later, I was deeply absorbed in editing the latest episode of our podcast. I had my headphones on, since Erica's mom was making supper in the kitchen. My office is in the living room, and there's no wall between the kitchen and the living room, so headphones are a requirement to get anything done when she's cooking.

Erica tapped me on the shoulder, startling me back into

reality. "Supper's ready. And we need to go back to the clinic around eight and check on Flecha."

I put my headphones on the desk and stretched. "How's she doing?"

"No change. The pain meds are helping but she still isn't very comfortable."

"They probably would have worked fine four days ago," I muttered. "Back when this should have been addressed."

After supper, we drove back to the clinic. It was after eight by then, and had been fully dark for several hours. My internal clock kept telling me it was time to get ready for bed, and I had to push through the jaw-splitting yawns. It's one of the hazards of being a morning person and marrying an equine veterinarian.

Flecha stood quietly in her stall, her head drooping near the floor. The four fluid bags hanging from the ceiling were nearly empty. I marveled again at how much she resembled a moose with her mane shaved off and her ears sagging. As short as the mane stubble was, it must have been clipped in the last day or two. I decided that was Debra's way of showing love to Flecha, grooming her when she was sick since she didn't have any other options.

Erica checked Flecha's vitals while I stood outside the stall and took notes. Flecha's eyes were half-closed, with lines of wrinkles across the top. That's a pain indicator in horses, along with a triangular, wrinkled nostril, and she was displaying both in a significant way.

"Heart rate is eighty. It hasn't really dropped below seventy all afternoon." She moved the stethoscope back to Flecha's belly. "Still no gut sounds. Let's put a tube in her and see if there's any reflux."

I grabbed the buckets and put a few inches of water in one of them. With the tube, pump, and bottle of lube in my other hand, I returned to the stall.

"I'm not questioning your doctor skills, but how would she have anything in her stomach?" I asked. "She's been on IV fluids all day, and we haven't tubed her with anything, right?"

"Right." Erica lubed the tube and began passing it up Flecha's nostril. "But dilution is the solution to pollution. If there's something going on in the gut, the body will pull all the fluid it can out of the blood, and from between cells, and dump it into the GI tract to try and flush out the problem. That's how diarrhea happens."

"So she can absorb twenty liters of fluids and still be dehydrated?"

"Yep. We've already pulled a bucket of fluids off her stomach once this afternoon. Be careful when you get the siphon going. If she's got a full stomach again, it'll probably come out fast."

She handed me the end of the tube, and I attached it to the pump. I worked the handle a few times, putting just enough water into the tube to fill it all the way to her stomach, then pulled it off the pump and pointed it into the empty bucket. I barely got it over the rim before a gush of green, horrible-smelling water came gushing out. It splashed off the bottom of the bucket and coated my arm and face in a fine spray, and I tried not to gag at the thought of what was on my lips and glasses.

Erica held the tube firm against Flecha's nose as she lifted her head up. Horses are physically incapable of vomiting, but sometimes they still need to, like now. Since her body wasn't moving the fluids out of the stomach, they were just piling up there, and it had to be a relief to have it removed. I kept the tube pointed at the bucket as she moved, and tried to breathe as little as possible.

When the stream finally stopped flowing, the bucket was nearly full. I emptied it, and washed everything, including myself, in hot, soapy water. When I was done, I went back to the stall where Erica stood watching Flecha through the open door.

"Well, what do you think?"

Erica shook her head. "Not good. I'm afraid she's going to rupture her gut. She's just not rallying like I'd hoped."

"Does that mean this is it?"

"Pretty much. I'm going to call the owners and see if they want to come here so we can euthanize her on the trailer so they can take her home and bury her, or how they want to do it. They're almost two hours north of here, so we gotta get this going now."

My temper pulsed dully in my head at the thought of Juan showing up here, and I immediately clamped down on it. No matter how much of a jerk he was, I couldn't be unprofessional. It was past my bedtime, and the best thing I could do was stand there and keep my mouth shut. Still, I sidled up beside Erica so I could hear what was said.

Debra answered on the third ring. "Hello?"

"Hey Debra, it's Dr. Lacher."

"Oh, hi. Is Flecha okay?"

"She's not good, I'm afraid. Her body just isn't responding to the fluids, and we can't get her pain under control. It's time to make some hard decisions."

"We need to euthanize her?"

"I think it's the right thing to do at this point. I wish I had a better answer."

I could hear muffled sobbing, and then a bit of Spanish as she explained the situation to Juan. A moment later, she was back. "Would surgery help her?"

Erica and I locked eyes in a moment of stunned rage. After four days of suffering without treatment, and a fight nine hours earlier about even running fluids on her, and just hours before she was likely to die on her own, Juan was ready to send her to surgery. I was incredibly glad Erica was on the phone and not me.

"At this point, it's a long shot," she said. "They might be able to do something, but it's probably going to cost over $20,000, with a low likelihood of a good outcome. So much time has passed now, it's hard to say."

There was another exchange in Spanish. This time the now-familiar sound of Juan shouting was a large part of it. Debra was pleading with him, but it didn't sound good, so I was surprised when she came back to us with a hopeful tone. "We're going to come pick her up and take her to Palm Beach," Debra said. "Juan knows a vet there that will give him a discount on surgery."

"Palm Beach? That's five hours south of here, and you guys are two hours north," Erica said. "If you're serious about sending her to surgery, she needs to be at a referral hospital within the hour. The only way that can happen is if we put her on our trailer and take her to Ocala right now. I don't think she would survive the trailer ride to Palm Beach."

There was another exchange in Spanish. It was all I could do to keep from banging my head against the wall. Juan was doing everything backwards, absolutely everything. If he was willing to send her to surgery now, why not nine hours ago? Why not four days ago? Four days ago it wouldn't have even been a discussion about surgery, most likely, because it wouldn't have been necessary. This nightmare was of his own making, and Flecha was dying because of his screwed-up thinking process.

"How much for you to haul her to Ocala?" Debra asked.

"Two hundred."

"Okay. What do we need to do?"

I didn't wait around to hear the rest of the conversation. I sprinted to the vet truck and drove home as fast as I dared. It took a full twenty minutes for me to get home, get the trailer hooked up to the truck, and get back to the clinic. Erica was waiting at the barn door with Flecha when I pulled up.

"Let's put her in the back slot," I said, flinging the doors open and dropping the ramp. "If she goes down in the trailer, it'll be a lot easier to get her up from there."

Erica led Flecha up the ramp, and she loaded without a fuss. By the time I had the trailer closed up, Erica had locked the clinic, and we hit the road. It was ten pm, and we had a forty-five-minute drive to get to the referral hospital in Ocala. I didn't even want to think about what time we would get home. I blamed Juan for that, too.

I stewed in silence as Erica spoke to the intern at the referral hospital and gave them the case history. Part of me was trying to understand Juan, and why he was so illogical in his approach to all of this, and so angry. Everything was a guess, as I was trying to psychoanalyze a person I knew almost nothing about, but I've learned a lot about my own insecurities, and how they've driven my behavior most of my life, so I could make a pretty good guess. When someone is being irrational and reacting with anger to everything, there's a lot more going on than what's on the surface. Knowing that Juan's behavior towards both his wife and mine, not to mention his attitude about his horse, was based on insecurities and low self-esteem did little to help me find empathy for him. I still mostly wanted to kick his ass.

At some point, I realized Erica had been off the phone for a while, and was over there brooding, just like me. "This has been going on for four days," I said, breaking the silence. "I know we don't even know what's wrong with her, exactly, but walk me through this timeline. If they had hauled it in on Day 2 instead of Day 4, what would have been different?"

Erica sighed. "Everything. Everything would have been different. When something goes wrong in the body, a countdown clock starts. In the beginning, the body is strong, and the problem is weak, whether it's a virus, or bacteria, or an impaction. As time goes by, that reverses. The body gets weaker, and the problem gets stronger. So the longer it goes, the harder it is to fix. Remember, the body is doing most of the work; we're just supporting it however we can."

"That's the same with humans, right?"

"It's the same with all biologic systems. Horse, human, cat, bird, fish, tree, grass, fungus."

We fell back into silence. The radio played quietly in the background as the miles ticked by. We passed through Williston without hitting any red lights, and I sped down the divided 4-lane highway towards Ocala as fast as I could without risking jail time. Eventually we turned on to Highway 326, and a few minutes later we arrived at the hospital.

The veterinarian and technician met us at the trailer as I opened the door and dropped the ramp. Flecha was still standing, to the relief of us all. The tech clipped the lead rope on and led her gently down the ramp and inside the hospital. I closed up the trailer while Erica completed the paperwork and talked to the other doctor.

"Alright, let's go home," Erica said as she climbed in the truck. She scrubbed her face for a moment and leaned back in the seat. As long as the day had been for me, it had been twice as long for her.

It was midnight before I got the trailer parked and staggered up to bed. Fortunately, I was too tired to lay awake and stew about Juan. I fell asleep almost immediately and didn't wake up until the donkeys started braying at seven the next morning. Before we even got out of bed, Erica got a text message from the surgeon at the referral hospital.

"They euthanized Flecha."

I had expected it to end this way, but it still hit me hard. "Did they do surgery on her?"

Erica shook her head. "No, they couldn't stabilize her enough to anesthetize her before she crashed. It was a race between her dying and them euthanizing her."

"Did they figure out what was going on with her?"

"No. They're guessing a colitis, but without a necropsy, there's no way to know."

There was no satisfaction for either of us about Erica being right about the severity of Flecha's condition. I wanted to rage at Juan, to shout at him that he had murdered his horse, that this was all his fault. I wanted to rub his face in it until he admitted what he had done. I wanted him to accept responsibility and change his ways to keep it from ever happening again. Wishful thinking.

Three hours later, Debra came into the clinic to pay

Flecha's bill. Her left eye was purple and swollen shut, and she tried to hide it behind her hair. Juan wasn't with her. She didn't say much, and didn't look anyone in the eye. When she got her receipt, she thanked us for trying to save Flecha, hung her head, and hurried out to her truck.

Mary, the receptionist, wiped a tear from her eye. "I feel like we should do something for her," she said. "I just don't know what to do."

I knew how she felt. "She's in a bad spot. I'm guessing that she stays there to take care of the horses, because he's obviously not going to. It's a horrible situation, but there's really nothing anyone can do other than let her know she has a safe place to go if she decides to leave him."

"I hope she makes it," Mary said faintly. "Lots of women don't."

I hoped she did, too. And I also hoped a satellite would fall out of space and land on Juan. What a flower.

4

23 Mollie

Our vet clinic has doubled in terms of staff in the eight years that I've been here, and nearly tripled in the number of horses that we take care of. That means things can get insanely busy, and I sometimes find myself pitching in and answering phones. That used to make me nervous, because I wasn't actually a horse person, and I didn't know enough about any of this to help clients. That's slowly changed over the years, and even though I still don't consider myself a horse person, I know a lot more than I used to. Part of it is six years of interviewing Erica on our podcast, and part of it's nine years of being married to a veterinarian, being on call with her, and running an equine veterinary clinic. I've picked up a few things along the way.

December 30th was a Friday, and everyone at the clinic was looking forward to a nice, quiet holiday weekend. We didn't have any patients in the hospital, so the two clinic cats were the only critters we needed to take care of. Erica was on call, but the weather was mild (a relief after the recent cold snap that froze the whole country, even here in Florida) and I didn't anticipate much excitement. How have I not learned by now that this is the exact recipe for chaos?

At 4:30 that afternoon, the phone rang, and I grabbed it. "Springhill Equine, this is Justin."

There was a pause on the other end. "Who is this again?"

"This is Justin."

"Oh, hi Justin. Sorry, I wasn't expecting a man to answer the phone, and it threw me off. Are you new?"

I laughed. "I hear that a lot. I'm not new, I just don't answer the phones a lot. I'm Dr. Lacher's husband."

"Oh, of course! You're *that* Justin! I listen to your podcast all the time; I should have recognized your voice! I'm sorry."

"It's nothing to be sorry about," I said. "What can I do for you?"

"This is Shelly Wilson, from Oak Hill Farm. I'm down in south Florida right now, and my barn manager just called me and said Mollie looks like she's about to foal. She's not due until January 16th, but she's waxing this afternoon. I was going to bring her in to you all to foal out next week, but is there any way she can come in today?"

Images of alarm clocks, hourly camera checks, and middle of the night false-alarm trips to the clinic raced through my mind, and my fantasy of a quiet New Year's weekend of reading and writing was shattered. But on the bright side, watching a new foal learn how to stand and nurse is an experience like no other.

"Of course," I said. "Do you have someone who can bring her in?"

"Yes, they can have her there in forty-five minutes. I'm texting Kristen now."

Once we hung up, I sent a message to the team over our group chat. *Mollie Wilson waxing up, coming in to foal out, will be here by 5pm.*

Before I could get out of the chair to go talk to the team, I heard startled exclamations coming from the other end of the clinic. It was instant bedlam.

"Foal out? It's still 2022, we can't have a foal yet!"

"Does anyone know where the pH strips are?"

"Which one is Mollie? Is that the sweet bay mare?"

"Do we even have any pH strips?"

"Do we have pelleted bedding?"

"We're not ready for foaling season! It's too soon!"

"We're going to need a camera watch all weekend."

"I don't even have the cameras on my phone, does anyone know how to set it up?"

Most of our breeding and foaling work happens between February and May, so everyone was rusty. Some of the techs ran out to the barn to get a stall ready, while others began making a list of necessary supplies and pulling it all together. We use pH test strips, the same ones you use to test your pool water, to test the mare's milk. When the pH drops to a certain range, it's a very strong indicator that the foal will be born that night. And of course, we didn't have any test strips on the shelf. At least that was something I could buy at the local hardware store.

By the time the mare arrived, we had ourselves mostly composed. The stall was bedded, the pH strips were acquired, the chart was printed, the stall camera was set, and everyone was briefed on the process. There was a sense of excitement in the air, as there always is at the beginning of foaling season. It would wear off over the coming months, but the first foal of the year was special.

Mollie was a beautiful bay quarter horse. I cast a critical eye over her feet as she walked in the barn, a habit I've formed over the years, and I was pleasantly surprised to see that they were well-trimmed. So many horses, and a lot of them expensive performance horses, have long toes, way too long. This keeps the tendons on the back of the leg stretched out and sets the horse up for a myriad of problems. An improperly balanced foot is the foundation for a lame horse, and it's the easiest thing in the world to prevent. We made a video for our YouTube channel that teaches horse owners how to check the balance of their horse's feet, and ever since then, I've become the world's biggest hoof critic. That gets reinforced every time we have a client horse retire ten years earlier than it should due to chronic lameness problems stemming from a lifetime of long toes. But I digress.

They started out by putting Mollie in the stocks to do a physical exam. She was so wide that her ribs rubbed the poles on both sides, and there was no doubt that she was very pregnant. Since it was the end of the day, the whole team was there to help out. Erica listened to her heart, breathing, and gut sounds while Jessie, one of the techs, worked on getting a drop of the mare's milk on a pH strip. That's a fairly simple procedure in theory, but it's awkward to do without putting yourself in a dangerous position until the mare gets used to it.

"Seven point oh," Jessie announced.

Dr. Lacher nodded. "Okay, so probably not tonight. We'll see what she is tomorrow. Dr. Hanks, how relaxed does she look under her tail?"

Dr. Hanks, one of our young new veterinarians, lifted Mollie's tail. "Um, pretty relaxed. But it looks like she's had a Caslick's procedure."

Erica pulled the stethoscope from her ears and walked to the back of the horse. "Well, that's probably going to need to come out, huh? Have you done one before?"

Dr. Hanks shook her head. "I've put two in with you, both back when I was a student, but I haven't removed one."

"Well, today's your lucky day," Erica said with a grin. "It's time to learn a new skill!"

A Caslick's procedure is a delicate thing to describe if you don't know what it is. I'll do my best here, but please extend me some grace on this. One of the many challenges of successful breeding in horses is infection. Horses have a conformational difficulty here, as the rectum is directly above the vulva. The vulva is the mare's first barrier against infection, and it has to keep fecal material and bacteria from getting inside. Because a horse's vulva is so big, this can be a really hard thing to achieve, especially for brood mares who have had multiple foals.

When a veterinarian performs a Caslick's procedure, they essentially sew the top third of the vulva shut. This decreases the risk of uterine infection significantly, while still allowing bodily functions to happen normally. However, when the mare is ready to have her foal, like now, the vulva has to be cut open back to its original size. Otherwise, there would be a massive bottleneck as the foal approached the opening, and something bad would happen.

Everyone crowded around as Dr. Lacher explained to Dr. Hanks how to open the Caslick's. Dr. Lacher demonstrated the process a few times, making sure Dr. Hanks knew what to watch out for.

"Your fingers are providing the support on the inside, but it's easy to focus on keeping your incision straight and forget about where your other hand is. You don't want to cut your finger. It's dual focus. Left hand inside, fingers wide and firm, keeping even pressure. Right hand is making a smooth, steady cut, bottom to top."

They numbed the area with lidocaine so Mollie wouldn't feel anything, and then Dr. Hanks traded places with Erica and did a few practice runs. "How do I know how high to go?"

"You can see the scar line running up there. That's the original apex, right where that ends. That's where we'll stop."

"Okay, got it."

Everyone fell silent, and Dr. Hanks picked up the scalpel. With the confidence of someone who had done it a thousand times, she made a perfect incision, and it was over in a few seconds. To be fair, she'd done a lot of surgeries on dogs and cats, so it's not as if she was completely inexperienced. Still, I admired her courage. She had all the makings of a really fantastic veterinarian, and I was happy to have her on the team.

With that done, Mollie headed off to her stall for a night of munching on hay and being miserably pregnant. Once she was settled in, we closed down the clinic for the long weekend. Even though her pH level indicated that tonight wasn't likely to be the night, we still set up a camera watch rotation. Every hour throughout the night, someone would check on her and call us if she was in labor.

Friday night passed without incident. As an early riser,

I took over the camera watch at four a.m. on Saturday, but Mollie barely moved. Saturday was much the same as Friday, and we welcomed in the New Year in my favorite way: sound asleep. On Sunday, her pH was still the same at breakfast, but the tech that fed her at dinner had the news we'd been waiting for. Erica's phone dinged the same time as mine with the announcement in the group chat.

Mollie's pH dropped to 6.5, tail is very soft, and she's pretty uncomfortable.

"Well, it looks like we're not going to get much sleep tonight," Erica said.

"Why can't horses foal in the daytime?" I asked. "I'm closing in on fifty. This late-night stuff is for young people. I'm going to talk to someone about this."

"Good luck with that," Erica said with a smirk.

At ten pm, I was just drifting off when the group chat buzzed again. I didn't open my eyes, but I knew right away that sleep was out of the question, at least for now.

"We gotta go," Erica said. "She's in labor."

"Tell her to wait until tomorrow," I mumbled.

Erica was already half dressed, so I dragged myself out of bed. Anytime a mare is foaling, there's always the threat of a red bag, which is a life and death situation for the foal. When that happens, the placenta cuts off oxygen to the foal before it's born, and it can suffocate. We can't risk that, so we always try to get to the clinic before the foal is born.

Erica pulled up the stall camera on her phone while I drove. The roads were empty of both vehicles and wildlife, which is just how I like it at night. Erica gave me status reports as the situation developed.

"She's standing up again. Hurry."

"I'm doing 75."

"It looks like the front feet are poking out, but she's at a bad angle to the camera. Hurry."

"I'm doing 85."

"We need a teleporter."

"I agree. Then I could stay in bed, and you could call me if you needed help." I smiled in the darkness, and she reached over and squeezed my arm.

"It's only six weeks until our vacation, you can take a nap then."

It took nine minutes to get to the clinic, but it seemed like twenty. The automatic gate slowly lumbered open, but Erica didn't wait for it. She hopped the fence, and had the clinic open and the lights on by the time I got parked. I met her in front of the stall.

Mollie was laying down again, and there were definitely front feet poking out. They pulsed in and out a few inches with her breathing, and they had already torn through the amniotic sac, so that was good. Mollie took a big breath and all four feet came off the floor as another intense contraction gripped her. The foal's feet slid out a few more inches, followed by a nose. I had forgotten all about being sleepy by this point.

The contractions were constant now, and the foal crept out bit by bit. The whole head slid out in one push, chin tucked neatly between the front legs. Mollie sucked in a giant lung full of air and held it, grunting with exertion as she pushed. The foal's shoulders came into view, and it slid more easily to the hips before stopping. Mollie blew out the breath she'd been holding and lay panting for a moment.

The foal raised its head, blinking under the stall lights.

Its front legs kicked a few times, as if trying to find the floor. The activity caused it to slide out another inch, and that small success seemed to inspire it to finish the birthing process all by itself. With front legs flailing and head swinging wildly, its hips came into view, and the front feet were able to touch the ground. It lay there for a moment, presumably getting ready for a second go. Suddenly, Mollie pushed up and lurched to her feet. As her back end came off the ground, the foal slid neatly out the rest of the way. The amniotic sac still covered it from the shoulders down, stretching up to the mare. Mollie took a step forward, and it tore in two. She turned around and began licking the foal, stripping the remains of the sac from its dark wet coat.

"Do we know if they have a name picked out?" I asked.

Erica shook her head. "No. We'll just go with the year and the mare's name. That's how everyone does it. This will be *23 Mollie* until they name it."

I pulled my phone out to take a picture and noticed that the group chat was going a mile a minute. It was a wonder the camera system hadn't crashed with ten people accessing it at the same time. I took a couple of pictures and posted them for everyone. The overhead view from the security cameras just isn't the same as seeing it from ground level.

Erica carefully entered the stall, moving slowly to avoid spooking Mollie. This was her first foal, and she was likely to be over-protective of it, just like a human mother with her first child. The foal was still laying down, but its head was up, jerking from point to point as it learned how to move everything. Erica squatted down and lifted its tail.

"It's a filly," she called out.

She stood up and moved to the back end of Mollie,

sliding her hand down her flank. The amniotic sac was dragging on the floor, collecting shavings, so she tied it up in a knot so it would hang halfway down. In the one, two, three rule, where the foal should be standing in one hour and nursing in two, the mare should pass the placenta in three hours. It was ten-thirty at night, so I really hoped it wouldn't take that long.

I put a message on the group chat so everyone would know it was a filly, along with a few more pictures. Now that the mare was getting it cleaned up, I could see that the foal was a bay with three white socks. She was soaking wet, so I couldn't tell how dark she would be.

Erica was still in the stall when the filly started scrambling, trying to stand. This is always a difficult thing to watch, second only to nursing for the first time. The stall mats and bedding make it hard for a foal to get traction as they're learning how to stand up. That's the tradeoff of foaling inside rather than outside. On the upside, you don't have to worry about other animals (like dogs or coyotes) getting involved, it's a cleaner environment, and you can watch them with the cameras.

The filly lunged a few times, feet sliding around, but she wasn't ready to actually stand up yet. Erica pushed some bedding around to try and help her get a better purchase. On the third try, Erica used her foot to brace the filly's front feet, and her hind end rose slowly into the air. Her back legs were wobbly, and her hips swung from side to side as she tried to figure out what to do with her front end. Mollie came around the side and nosed her baby on the stomach, lifting her front end up. Erica moved her foot with the filly as she made her way upright, keeping her toes braced. At last, she stood on her own, weaving around like the town drunk, but she was doing it all by herself.

Erica slipped out of the stall and stood beside me. We watched as Mollie continued to groom her foal, who was struggling to remain upright with all the licking. All at once, she collapsed in a heap.

"Well, that was the end of round one," I said with a chuckle.

"I'm going to text the owner," Erica said. "Can you give me a couple of pictures to send her?"

I sent her three pictures showing the progression from being freshly born to standing, and she fired off the birth announcement.

Round two happened about five minutes later and went much better. By now, Mollie had the foal reasonably clean, and she was beginning to dry. It was still too early to make a firm color call, but I was leaning towards chestnut. She staggered around the stall on experimental legs, taking her first real steps only forty minutes after being born.

The next hurdle was nursing, my least favorite part of foaling. Having watched this process dozens of times, I expected the foal to have a hard time figuring it out, and she didn't disappoint. At first, she kept looking on the wrong end of the mare, jamming her head between the front legs. I don't know if Mollie was trying to help, or was just walking away, but every time this happened, she went to the other side of the stall. Finally, after four rounds of this, the foal got to the business end of the breakfast bar. She still couldn't find the udder, but at least she was in the ballpark.

After ten long, unsuccessful minutes of trying to nurse, the foal gave up and crumpled to the floor in a heap. To my surprise, she didn't fall asleep, she just sat there and looked around. I checked the time. It was right at sixty minutes post birth, so she was still well within the window for nursing, but nearly every foal I had watched previously had consumed at least a little bit of milk before their first nap. Not that she was napping, though. She was still looking around, her head jerking clumsily from one point to another.

"That's a little weird, huh?" I glanced at Erica. "She's not really doing things wrong, but it doesn't seem quite right, either."

Erica shrugged. "I don't know. It's too early to say."

I didn't push it. My threshold for risk is much lower than Erica's, and so is my level of knowledge and experience. If she was comfortable with how things were going, I needed to work on getting there, too.

At seventy minutes, the foal climbed to her feet again. It took a couple of tries, but she got there on her own. Just like the first time, she went to Mollie's chest and tried to find a place to nurse. Mollie stepped away, the placenta swinging behind her like a pendulum. The foal moved into the udder and began trying to latch on.

"Come on, kiddo," I whispered. "You can do it!"

Minutes passed; long, painful minutes, and the foal still couldn't find the right spot. Just when I couldn't take it anymore, Erica gave up and opened the stall door.

"Alright, filly. Let's get you some milk before you run out of energy." Erica guided the foal's head toward the udder with one hand, and grabbed a teat with the other, spraying a fine stream of milk on the filly's muzzle. This ramped up the filly's enthusiasm to feed, but it also made it harder for Erica to help. Finally, once everyone was covered in milk and sweat, the sounds of gurgling and swallowing filled the stall. Success!

She didn't nurse long, maybe four or five good swallows before she stepped back, but it was a start. Erica wiped the milk off her muzzle before leaving the stall. We watched as she walked a few laps around Mollie, her leg and head movements still awkward and twitchy. She laid down again for a few minutes but got back up without actually sleeping.

"She's almost ninety minutes in," I said. "She's had five swallows of milk and hasn't slept at all. What's the line that makes you concerned?"

The words were barely out of my mouth when the foal started on her second round of successful nursing. After another five or six swallows, she backed up and walked away. Suddenly she stopped in her tracks, staring at the wall with intense focus. Her little tail raised straight up, her back legs spread apart a few inches, and a moment later her first poop hit the floor. It was thick and black, a substance called meconium, and it was another important waypoint that Erica had been waiting for.

"She's not doing everything perfect, but she's still doing all the stuff." She grabbed a pitchfork and slipped into the stall to pull the meconium out before anyone stepped in it. "I'm not too worried yet, but we're going to keep a close eye on her."

Over the next few hours, the foal alternated between walking around, nursing, and napping. Once I saw her actually go to sleep, I began to feel better about her. Mollie passed the placenta without issue around the two-hour mark, and after Erica examined it for any missing pieces or signs of problems, I took it out back and buried it in the compost pile. At 1:30 am, we finally went home. I set the alarm for 6:00 am, knowing I was going to be a zombie when it went off.

When I got to the clinic the next morning, most of the doctors and techs were gathered at the fence beside one of the paddocks. Mollie was munching on hay, with the foal standing off to one side. I hurried over to see what I was missing.

"I don't think it's the wrong answer," Erica was saying. "I think we squeeze her now, and if she doesn't look better by noon, we ship her to the referral hospital."

I knew right away that the foal was still not quite right. The Madigan Squeeze is a technique veterinarians use on dummy foals, which is a term for foals who don't seem to get the hang of nursing and napping right away. The technical term is *Neonatal Maladjustment Syndrome.* When foals are born, the process of going through the birth canal squeezes them, and that triggers certain processes in the brain, like eating and running around, which weren't happening before. Sometimes they can successfully replicate that squeeze on a dummy foal and get it to start behaving normally. A tiny part of me was excited that I'd recognized that something was wrong with the foal the night before, but most of me was sad that it was happening.

"Justin, can you haul them to Ocala if it comes to that?" Erica asked.

I pulled out my phone and glanced over my calendar. "Yep, can do."

"Okay. Let's get to work."

The squeeze is performed by wrapping a rope around the foal's torso in a very specific pattern. Erica adjusted the rope placement a few times until she was satisfied, then started tightening it down.

"The foal's going to lay down," she said. "Make sure Mollie can see her, but don't let her come over and get on top of us."

The techs got out of the way, and a moment later, the foal slowly dropped to the grass. Erica followed her down, keeping the pressure on the rope just right. It was as if she had flipped a light switch on the foal. It was asleep within seconds, and the two of them stayed there for twenty minutes. Mollie continued to eat hay, glancing over occasionally to check on her baby.

"Time," Dr. Hanks announced. "That's twenty minutes."

Erica slowly released the pressure on the rope. I knew she had to be sore from holding it, but she didn't let it show. When the rope was removed, everyone stepped back. A few seconds later, the foal raised her head and looked around, then climbed to her feet.

"Alright, let's get out of here and see how she does," Erica said. "We ought to see a difference pretty quick."

By the time we were all out and the gate was shut, the foal was nursing. Dr. Hanks and her tech left to go see their next appointment, and I moved down the fence to stand beside Erica.

"What all are we watching for?" I asked.

"I mainly want to see her be a little more energetic," Erica said. "She's been standing still, just acting too quiet. She should be running around annoying her mom by now. Cassie's running an IgG test to see if she got enough colostrum overnight, which I doubt she did, but I want to see her acting more like a toddler and less like an old man."

"What happens if she didn't get enough colostrum?"

"We'll give her some plasma and ship her to the hospital."

I glanced at my watch. "I guess I should head back to the house and get the trailer hooked up, just in case. How long will it take you to run a bag of plasma?"

"Probably half an hour."

Both of our phones dinged at the same time as a Chat message came in.

IgG is 6.

"Normal is eight, right?" I asked.

Erica nodded. "It's a little low, but not horrible. Four is the panic number. I think we'll get her through this, but she's going to need a lot of support. The owner's on board to ship her down to Ocala, so let's go ahead and do it. We'll have the plasma in her by the time you get back with the trailer."

It took me twenty-five minutes to get to the house and back, and I had managed to get myself in a fair state of anxiety by then. Hauling foals is one of the most stressful things in the world. Hauling a foal that hasn't even been standing a full day yet is twice as bad. They have rickety balance, minimal fine motor control, and no experience on a trailer. It's a recipe for disaster.

Mollie loaded right up on the trailer, and the techs boosted the foal up behind her and closed the door. I'm sure the people behind me thought I was crazy as I drove, but I feathered the brake as lightly as possible coming up to every red light and corner. My approach was to imagine a tower of wine glasses in the trailer, and my mission was to get to the referral hospital without any of them falling. The last thing I wanted was for the foal to end up with a concussion or a broken leg on top of everything else.

As I pulled out of Archer and headed towards Williston, an SUV whipped out from behind me and went racing past. I was already up to 50 mph, but I had accelerated slowly, so I wasn't surprised that he wanted around. What caught me off guard five seconds later was when he slammed on the brakes and put his left turn signal on.

"What are you doing?" I shouted, stepping on the brake as hard as I dared. There was a truck coming towards us, and I didn't think there was time for the SUV to turn before it got to us. I also didn't have time to feather the brake and do a slow stop. I spent a nanosecond debating about driving off onto the grass shoulder to go around, and whether that would be more dangerous for the foal than slamming on the brakes. Before I could decide which way to go, the SUV turned. The oncoming truck slammed on the brakes, honking his horn as he veered into my lane momentarily to avoid clipping the back end of the SUV.

A moment later it was all over. The SUV was gone, the truck was gone, and I was shaking like a leaf. I desperately wanted to follow the SUV and beat some sense into the driver. Instead, I took my foot off the brake pedal and went on down the road while trying to coach myself through some anger management. I decided not to pull over and check on the foal. If she was hurt, the only thing I could do to help would be to get her to the hospital, and pulling over would only slow us down from getting there. Mollie wasn't raising a ruckus, so I took that as a good sign and grimly pressed on.

The rest of the journey passed without incident. I was still mad when I got out of the truck at the hospital, but my hands had stopped shaking, so that was an improvement. A group of veterinarians, technicians, and vet students met me at the back of the trailer. Dr. Davis stepped over to greet me.

"Hi, Justin! Is this 23 Mollie?"

I nodded. "Sure is. I wasn't expecting such a big welcoming committee."

She shrugged. "Well, it's our first foal of the year, so everyone's excited."

"I had to slam on the brakes on the way here, and I don't know if she went down or not." I unlatched the door.

"Got it. We'll get them off the trailer and check them both out."

I carefully opened the door, dreading what might be waiting on the other side. Instead of a sea of broken legs, a soft nose immediately poked out as the foal surveyed her new surroundings with wide eyes. Mollie nickered softly from the front slot, and the foal gave a tiny high-pitched whinny in reply. A chorus of oohs and ahs emanated from the group behind me, and I stepped out of the way and let them do their job. A minute later, Mollie and her foal were walking into the referral hospital, both seemingly healthy and uninjured. I breathed a sigh of relief.

After signing all the necessary paperwork, I climbed back in the truck and headed home. Of course, no one made me slam on the brakes now that I had an empty trailer. I caught myself ruminating about it over and over on the drive back, despite my best efforts to change the subject in my head. At last, I pulled a mental image of my therapist into the conversation, and that helped me find some peace with it. I decided to use it as a reminder to be more patient with other people who are holding me up when I'm in a hurry. After all, I don't know what's going on with them any more than the jerk in the SUV knew that I had a brand new foal in the trailer.

Mollie and her foal ended up staying at the hospital in Ocala for several days. The foal got another round of plasma, along with some medications and lots of fluids to help her catch up to where she should be. Erica got regular updates on them, and on Thursday, they were released to go home. I had just arrived at the clinic when Erica got the call from Dr. Davis.

"Mollie and foal are being discharged," Erica announced. "The foal is doing great!" Everyone in the clinic cheered.

"Do I need to go pick them up?" I asked, fervently hoping that the answer would be no.

"No, the owner is going to get them."

I breathed a sigh of relief.

"In other news, we have another pregnant mare coming in this afternoon to foal out," Erica continued. "We need to get a stall ready."

Like everything else, the cycle continued on at the clinic. 23 Mollie was off at her own farm now, growing and learning how to be a horse. Another foal would come in and take our attention for a time, and then something else would happen. That's just the way it goes at a veterinary clinic. The trick is to enjoy the moment with whatever animal is in front of you. It's not any different than life with people, really.

5

Lessons Learned Hard are Lessons Learned Best

It was a Saturday morning in July, one of those hot, humid days that make Florida famous. The overnight low had only gone down to seventy-eight degrees, and it was back up in the mid-eighties by ten a.m. with the humidity over ninety percent. An all-around lovely day to stay inside; also, a great time to go see an emergency.

"The McCaskin foal managed to tear off an eyelid again," Erica said, poking her head inside the front door. The warm damp air from outside raced across the room and wrapped around me like a wet blanket.

"Isn't that the one we saw a few months ago for an eyelid?" I asked.

"One and the same, but this time it's the other eye."

"Well, there's that," I said. "Better now than this afternoon." I told myself that all the time, but I wasn't sure if it was true. The morning temperatures were lower, but the humidity was really high. In the afternoon the temperature would be higher, but the humidity would go down a little. It was hard to say which was better.

The McCaskin farm was north of Alachua, a little over twenty minutes from our house. It was a strange combination of nice and dumpy, and seemed to belong in a Larry McMurtry novel like *Texasville*. The long driveway led across a hundred acres of green pasture to a nice brick house and a white picket fence. But there was junk everywhere; an abandoned riding mower in the middle of a pasture, a kid's bicycle with a missing tire, a truck axle lying beside the dirt road in the weeds, an old washing machine on its side, that kind of stuff. And cows. Everywhere.

The mare and foal were in a corral built from portable panels next to the house, just outside the picket fence. The last blade of grass had been consumed years before, and there was a huge hole on one end. I couldn't decide if it was an out-of-control roll pit, or a swimming pool project that was never completed. The other end of the makeshift corral was covered by a carport. I pulled up as close as I dared, terrified of running over an old roll of barbed wire, or a baby cow taking a nap. We grabbed our supplies, closed the hatch to keep the cows out of the vet truck, and walked the last twenty feet to the horse pen.

"Should we text April that we're here?" I asked as I unclipped the chain from the corner panel.

Erica shook her head. "She's not here. She was leaving for something when she saw the eyelid."

On my previous trip here, April had not been helpful. I learned in the first five minutes that she loved barrel racing, had just graduated high school, planned to buy and breed eight mares in the coming year, and didn't know anything at all about horses. At that time, her foal was two months old, and we could tell right away that she wasn't handling it on a regular basis to get it accustomed to people. Erica had talked to her about training it, and I desperately hoped she had listened. Foals are hard to hold for the vet on their best behavior, and this one had been mostly wild. I remembered being annoyed as April stood by the fence telling us about her breeding plans while I was trying to hold the filly's head still enough for Erica to sew its eyelid back on.

There was a lead rope draped over the fence, but no halter. Remembering where I was, I looked around on the ground. A few feet outside the fence, I found a muddy rope halter. It was for an adult horse, but it would have to do. There was no foal halter to be found. My hopes of foal training were diminishing by the second.

"Let's leave the tray here until we catch this thing," Erica said. "This is probably going to be a two-person operation."

The mare was under the carport eating hay from the remains of a round roll, and completely ignored us. The foal was nursing when we came in but moved to the other side of the hay bale as we approached. Her left eyelid was poking out at a ninety-degree angle, and was covered in bloody dirt. I eased around the right side of the hay, gently pushing her towards Erica.

At first, I thought it was going to be easy, but the filly was just lulling me into a false sense of security. She stood quietly for a moment, then let out a little foal squeal, bucked twice, and shot past me. She ran to the other end of the corral, spun around, and raced back, then doubled back again, bucking and squealing. The mare didn't even flick an ear.

"Just let her run off some energy," Erica said, moving to the fence. "She'll calm down in a minute."

I didn't share her optimism, but there wasn't anything else to do. We watched her run back and forth, pausing on occasion to look at the cows on the other side of the fence who were staring at her. Finally, she went back to the mare and began nursing again.

"Okay, showtime." Erica grabbed the rope halter and moved to the left side of the mare. "You stay on the right, but don't pressure her."

I moved into position, holding my arms out a bit to show that the road was closed in this direction. To my surprise, Erica was able to walk up to her and slip the halter around her neck, where she tied it like a collar.

"See there, kiddo?" Erica said, handing me the lead rope. "That wasn't so bad. Let's go over here away from your mom and get a look at your eye."

The foal walked with me for a few steps, but then she tried to run again. I was ready for her, though, and held on to the rope. She ran in circles around me until I shortened the rope enough to get a hand on the halter. Once I got my other hand on her muzzle, I was able to get her stopped, and I quickly reached under her chin and grabbed her ear on the opposite side. I held her tail with my other hand, lifting it straight up. She danced around, but I was able to keep her under enough control for Erica to get a needle in her neck and give her a sedative. Once it was in, I released the hold and went back to the lead rope while we waited for the drugs to kick in.

As soon as I let go, she went back to running. She seemed content to run in a circle around me, so I just stood where I was, turning with her. We made four or five revolutions before a cow walked up to the fence. The foal stopped and sniffed the cow, then went back to running. After a few more laps, she slowed to a walk, her head drooping.

"There we go," I said. "I think she's getting into the happy place."

Erica walked back to the corner of the pen and grabbed the tray, and I reeled the foal in again. We met in the middle of the pen and got to work. I got back in the foal management position, holding the head and the tail, and Erica started cleaning the eyelid.

"Why did you have to roll in the dirt, kid?" She squirted saline on the area, and the mud slowly washed away. "This would have been a lot better if you'd kept it clean."

"I don't think that's ever a factor for a horse," I said. "Self-preservation isn't really a thing for them, except when talking about plastic bags." Plastic bags are universally terrifying for horses, a fact which is just as ridiculous to me now as it was when I learned about it nine years ago.

"I can't argue with you there."

Once the area was clean, Erica pulled up a syringe of Lidocaine. I tightened my grip on the ear and tail and braced myself. As expected, the filly began to fight and throw her head as soon as the needle touched her.

"Seriously," Erica said, smacking the foal on the nose. "I'm trying to numb it up. Give me three seconds."

I tightened my grip even more, but a five-month-old

horse is strong. I was also bent over, so she had a position advantage on me. Erica's nose tap bought us a few seconds of reprieve, but she was only able to get a bit of the drug into the filly before she began fighting us again.

"She must have a crazy high tolerance for sedation," I grunted. "Are you sure that's what you gave her?"

Erica stepped back. "I did, but it wasn't enough. Let me run back to the truck and get some more. We're never going to get it done like this."

She headed back to the truck, and I released the foal. As soon as I stepped back, she began running in circles again. I shook my head with a chuckle. As annoying as it was to try and work on her, I couldn't help but admire her independent spirit.

The cow at the fence poked its nose through the bars, and the filly stopped to stiff it. They both jumped back from the contact, and we were back to running laps. I turned with her, keeping a good grip on the rope. She was running a little slower with the sedation on board, but she still had way more enthusiasm than she should have at that point. She stopped again, facing away from me, and I paused in my circle, waiting for her to take off again.

I had a sudden urge to get to a bathroom, like a severe diarrhea cramp. That was confusing, as it came out of nowhere. I hadn't eaten anything unusual that I could think of. It wasn't that kind of feeling after all, I realized. It was a vomit cramp. How could I have confused those two things? They're quite different sensations. But why would I need to throw up? It was very strange.

It occurred to me that my eyes were closed, and just as I opened them, a lightning bolt of pain shot through me. It was overwhelming. My vision was hazy, but my focus was on the pain. It felt like it was coming from everywhere, but at least I wasn't about to puke my guts out anymore. I took a shallow breath, then another. The intensity of the pain receded slightly, enough for me to sense that it was coming from my right leg.

I blinked a few times, and my vision cleared. I was standing in a corral. I could see Erica at the vet truck, maybe a hundred yards away. At the fence between me and her, a foal was standing there with a lead rope dangling from the rope halter around its neck. It all came rushing back to me, where I was and what I'd been doing, and I finally realized what must have happened. The foal had kicked me, hard enough that I'd grayed out for a minute. That had never happened to me before.

My right leg felt like it had been shot with a cannon. I immediately assumed the worst, that my femur was shattered, and probably with shards of bone poking out of my leg like a pin cushion. Putting weight on it was not an option, and I was afraid that if I tried, I'd probably pass out and fall on it, exacerbating the problem. I looked down to see if I was bleeding, and realized my hand was still sticking out like I was holding the lead rope.

Fortunately, I was wearing shorts, so it was easy to determine that I didn't have a leg bone sticking through the skin. I was still woozy, and I didn't know how much longer I could stand there on one leg, and Erica was still at the vet truck. I didn't have enough gusto to shout at her, so I opted for the next best plan: try to get to the fence.

Now that I'd had a minute to collect myself and assess my leg, I was feeling a bit more in control. I hopped forward tentatively, testing the pain response. It was bearable, so I did it again, and a third time. Each impact sent a little lightning bolt up my leg, but not so bad that I couldn't handle it. Two more hops got me to the fence, and I grabbed on to it like a drowning man hugging a piece of driftwood.

I could feel my pulse in my leg. It throbbed with each heartbeat, a hot, stabbing pain over and over. Despite my best efforts as a kid, I'd never had a broken bone (knock on wood), so I didn't know how to tell how serious my injury was. Erica has been kicked in both quads by full-grown horses, and I knew she had massive muscle trauma from those injuries, but no broken femur. That made me question whether a foal was strong enough to break my leg. The pain said yes, but my slowly returning sensibilities said probably not.

The clanging chain announced Erica's return. I glanced over as she walked up, unwilling to release my hold on the fence.

"She got away from you, huh? I can't believe the sedation didn't slow her down any more than that."

I tried to respond. In my head, I said, *she kicked the shit out of me, and I think my leg's broken.* What came out of my mouth was more of a gasp and a bit of drool.

"Are you okay?" She looked at me sharply, her brow furrowing. "Why are you being weird?"

I took a shallow breath and tried again. "She kicked me." It came out as a weak whisper, but at least it came out.

In an instant, Erica transformed in a way I'd never seen before, or since. She was simultaneously furious and nurturing. I knew I shouldn't have let the foal turn her back on me, but I was way past defending myself for that rookie mistake. I hoped that this didn't mean Erica was going to fire me as her weekend emergency technician. It wasn't until her next statement that I realized her anger was directed at the foal, not at me, and then I felt silly.

"I'm going to kill that foal. Where did she get you?"

I pointed to my right leg. "Just above the knee."

She dropped down and lifted the leg of my shorts up. There was an angry red welt about three inches above my kneecap in a perfect foal footprint. I realized how lucky I was. If it had been a direct hit on my knee, my life would have been drastically different in that moment. And if it had been two inches higher, it would have been a direct hit on my phone, which would have cost me a thousand dollars.

"Can you put weight on it?"

I tightened my grip on the fence, ready for another lightning bolt of pain as I slowly leaned over. It hurt, but not in the blinding way it had before. I bent my knee, exploring the pain, but it wouldn't go more than a little bit. "It's crazy stiff, and it hurts like nobody's business, but I can put weight on it." My voice was getting stronger, too.

"That's good. Let me see if I can get the vet truck over here, and we'll get you sitting."

"What about the foal?" I asked.

"I'll see if one of the techs can come help me, or one of the other doctors."

I shook my head. "No, I can get through this. If you can grab her and get her over here, I'll be okay. Once we get her sedated, it won't be a big deal."

Erica looked doubtful. "Are you sure?"

I nodded. "You finished a dental on a horse after it kicked you. I can at least hold a foal." I'd never be as tough as Erica, but I had to at least try to stay within sight of her achievements.

We waited a few more minutes for my strength to return. I couldn't believe that a young foal had TKO'd me with a kick to the leg. It was embarrassing. But it was more embarrassing that I'd forgotten the fundamentals that Erica had drilled into me. Never get behind a horse. Never trust a horse you don't know. Never underestimate the strength of a horse, no matter how small it is. Complacency is what gets you hurt or killed. And here I was.

I shouldered the sweat from my forehead and took a test step on my right leg. It hurt, but it held. "Okay, let's get this done so I can get home and ice this thing."

Erica caught the foal, and I resumed the chin and tail hold, although mostly on one leg. She helped me stabilize the head with one hand and stuck the needle in with the other hand, hitting the vein on the first try. "If that doesn't slow her down, she's just going to have to grow a new eyelid."

"You're such a showoff." I tried to grin, but it turned into a grimace as I stood up.

"What are you talking about?"

"Hitting the vein one-handed on the fly. You make it look easy."

She shrugged. "It's what I do all day, every day."

This time, the foal's head went to her knees, and her legs were wobbly. Instead of holding her down, my job was going to be to hold her up. I tried a few different poses before I found one that I could hope to maintain for a few minutes. It mostly consisted of me holding her head up while we leaned against each other for balance; her on three legs and me on one. It wasn't pretty, but it worked.

Erica didn't mess around. Once I got in position, she quickly numbed the area and stitched the eyelid back in place. It was done in less than two minutes.

"Okay, let's get you out of here," Erica said. She grabbed the tray of supplies in one hand and wrapped her other arm around my waist. I untied the halter and tossed it over by the fence. If the owner wasn't worried about keeping it out of the dirt, I wasn't either. The foal just stood there with her head hanging. She might have had an eyelid injury, but she wasn't feeling any pain. I felt a twinge of envy.

We slowly hobbled to the truck, stopping to rest a few times along the way. It was hard on my pride to accept help, and I tried to remember all the things my therapist had taught me about that. Needing help was not a value judgment of my character. No one else would think I was weak or pathetic in that situation, and I shouldn't think those things about myself. Instead, I should be grateful that I have an amazing wife who loves me, and I shouldn't rob her of the opportunity to be needed. By the time we got to the passenger door, I had talked myself through it and was feeling pretty good about the whole situation.

"Watch your head." Erica gripped my forearm and eased me down into the seat. I lifted my left leg in, and we both lifted my right leg. As soon as it left the ground, the pain shot straight through me, and I moaned in spite of my efforts to be stoic. At last, my foot was on the floorboard, and I leaned back with a sigh of relief. Erica leaned across me and buckled my seatbelt, and I gave her a quick kiss on the cheek.

"Thanks for taking care of me," I said. "Earlier, I thought you might have to euthanize me, but now I think I'll be okay with a leg amputation."

She closed my door with a chuckle.

Halfway home, I realized what lay in store for me. We

lived on the second floor, and the only way up was the stairs. Fourteen steps, to be exact. I ran through my options. One, I could stay in a hotel. Impractical and expensive, but a possible solution. Two, I could create a makeshift living space in the tack room. There was no bathroom on the ground floor, so I immediately discarded that one. Three, I could climb the stairs. And honestly, if I could hold the foal and then walk to the truck, I should be able to climb the stairs. Sometimes I just have to reason things out with myself.

When we got home, my leg was so stiff I couldn't hardly get it out the truck door, but the pain had receded significantly. Erica helped me stand up, and once I was there, it was pretty manageable. Even climbing the stairs wasn't nearly as bad as I'd feared. I went slow, and used the rail, and it was okay. I iced it off and on throughout the afternoon, and stayed upstairs.

The next day, instead of being purple and unusable, as I'd anticipated, my leg was almost normal. It was sensitive to the touch, of course, but I was able to walk just fine. Even going downstairs to feed was okay. It was sore, but not debilitating. I had dodged a major bullet in terms of serious injury, and I'd learned a big lesson in the process: *Never get complacent*. Also, I apparently have a low threshold for pain, since a foal knocked me out, so that was even more reason to not take unnecessary risks. Erica might have survived two kicks from full-grown horses, but I wasn't sure I could handle it. I definitely didn't want to try!

6

We've Got a Runner!

Erica and I don't get dressed up very often. We rarely go places that expect it, so it's not that we show up dressed poorly at nice events, just to be clear. In the nine years that we've been together, I can only think of a few times where we really got spiffed up. There was a wedding, a vet school graduation, another wedding, and a funeral. Nearly everything we do involves animals in some way, which usually means hair, blood, and poop, and that stuff doesn't go very well with nice clothes. And fancy galas don't really excite either of us, anyway.

After I wrote *The Righteous Rage of a Ten-Year-Old Boy*, I began appearing as a guest on a lot of podcasts to talk about things like overcoming child abuse, active self-discovery, recovery from alcoholism, and things like that. Since most of these were video as well as audio, I had to ramp up my collection of nice shirts, which had been a total of one going into all that. I found out that I kind of liked wearing nice clothes and looking tidy and professional, even if it was only in our living room in front of the camera.

Since my lifestyle doesn't lend many opportunities to wear those things, I have to take what I can get. So it was that one Wednesday evening, Erica and I were headed to a dinner with one of our drug company representatives and her supervisor, which is how they get us to sit still and listen to a spiel about new products that are coming on the market. It wasn't really a fancy affair, but it was an opportunity to wear one of my nice shirts, and I took it.

We were driving through a rural area outside of Gainesville. The mid-summer sun was still high in the sky, and it reflected off the windshield of a delivery van down the road as it pulled out of a side street and turned towards us. The glare was intense, and left spots in my vision after the van finally went by. I was still blinking when Erica grabbed my arm.

"Stop! Stop! Oh, crap!"

There were no other vehicles on the road, so I had no idea what she was talking about, but the intensity of her shout left no room for argument. I slammed on the brakes and felt the ultrasound machine hit the back of my seat with a thud. As the vet truck shuddered to a stop, a miniature horse and a donkey ran out of the shadows on the side road in front of us and trotted across the highway, and immediately began grazing on the grass next to the fence. The mini was a brown and white paint, while the donkey was white and looked very similar to our Hannah Banana. If Erica hadn't spotted them, I very likely would have run right over them, and the thought made me sick to my stomach.

I looked in the mirror as Erica jumped out of the passenger seat. There was no one behind us, so that was good. I put the transmission in park and turned on the emergency flashers as Erica opened the hatchback and grabbed the halter and lead rope.

"I'm a little nervous about parking right in the road," I called out. Erica didn't answer. I peered in the mirror and spotted her on the other side of the highway. Leaving the vet truck in the road would slow down approaching traffic, which would be helpful, but assuming we caught the runaway critters, we would be leaving it behind as we walked them down the dirt road to wherever they came from. That was enough to convince me, and I pulled off on the shoulder.

If you've read the first book in this series, then you know about my experience chasing donkeys. It's not good. Unlike horses, who will cluster together for safety, donkeys understand the principle of divide and conquer. They know how to put out minimal effort in a way that will make you put out maximum effort. I was not going to underestimate this donkey.

Minis are a whole different creature. Much like small dogs, most of them don't take direction well, especially from a stranger. They also have a low center of gravity, which means they can turn sharp. We had to catch these two and get them back home safely, but I was under no illusions that it was going to be easy.

Erica had the only halter and lead rope on the truck, so

I grabbed the rope off the head loop that we use for dentals. It was about fifteen feet long, and would work in a pinch. I jogged down the shoulder past the side road and crossed the highway so the donkey and the mini were between me and Erica. There was still no traffic in sight: so far, so good.

With loose horses, there's a fifty-fifty chance that you can just walk up and put a halter on them. After all, that's an everyday occurrence for a lot of them. For most donkeys and minis, that's something that only happens when the vet or farrier comes, if it happens at all. You can walk up to our donkeys all day long provided you're empty-handed or carrying a food bucket, but the instant they see a halter, they're gone. Knowing that, I wasn't surprised that the mini shot across the road as soon as we started to approach.

If the donkey had followed the mini back across the highway, that would have been hugely helpful. Then it would have just been a matter of getting them headed back down the dirt road, where they would at least be safe from cars driving by at sixty miles an hour. Instead, the donkey turned towards me and feinted to its left as if it was going to shoot the gap between me and the fence. I fell for it, and as soon as I committed my weight in that direction, it twisted and slipped past me on the other side.

I spun around, feeling clumsy and slow after being so deftly outmaneuvered. The donkey hadn't gone far before stopping to graze again, maybe twenty feet. But now it was in front of me, and the dirt road was behind me. Erica was in the same position on the other side of the road with the mini. This was getting worse instead of better. I wiped the sweat from my forehead, trying to keep it off my nice purple shirt.

A vehicle came over the rise in the distance. I waved my

arms to try and get their attention and moved up to the edge of the road. If I could keep the donkey off the pavement until the car went by, then I could circle around and get on the other side and push it back in the right direction. The donkey stayed put near the fence, watching me as it munched on the recently mown grass. I turned to wave again, but there was no need. Blue and red lights were flashing on the roof, and it was stopping. Reinforcements had arrived!

The deputy pulled off the road and climbed out. He was tall and lanky like me, with a shock of dark brown hair and a thin mustache, and looked to be in his late twenties.

"Is this your donkey?" he asked.

I shook my head. "No, we were just driving by. We saw a delivery van come out of this road, and they were following it, so I'm guessing he left a gate open. My wife is over there trying to catch the mini horse."

He glanced down the road, then back to the donkey. "Do you all know anything about animals? Can you just walk up and grab it?"

"My wife is actually a horse veterinarian, so we deal with these things all the time. But no, they're not letting us catch them. Best bet is to push them back down the dirt road. It'll be way easier with a third person. Just hold your arms out to the side, like this, and try not to let them come back past you."

I put my arms out to demonstrate and sidled down past the donkey. As soon as I approached, it turned around and started walking down the shoulder. The deputy said something into his radio, then mirrored my action, staying up higher near the road.

"I'm going to try and get it off the fence and across the

pavement," I said. "It looks like Erica has the mini coming back this way, so maybe they'll group up for us."

After checking for traffic, I moved over next to the fence. The donkey turned up toward the road, and I got behind it, softly shooing it on. The mini was on the opposite shoulder, just past the dirt road, and whinnied as we came across the pavement. Erica moved towards me, forming a loose semi-circle around them. The donkey picked up a trot and made a beeline for the mini, and I felt a moment of relief. It didn't last long.

Instead of a joyful reunion where they both turned down the dirt road and headed for home, which was my vision, the donkey went right on by the mini and headed down the opposite side of the highway. Erica made a dash to cut it off, but she was too far away.

"Let's get the mini going down the dirt road," I shouted. "Maybe the donkey will follow."

We advanced on the mini, our arms out and waving. It squealed and bucked once, then turned and cantered down the dirt road. Erica and the deputy continued to push it, and I circled back around to try and get the donkey to follow them. As I got back up to the pavement, I saw a twinkle of sunshine reflecting off another approaching vehicle. It was big, clearly a tractor trailer. The distinct sound of the engine brake told me it was slowing down, and I was grateful to have the sheriff's SUV sitting there with the lights flashing.

I jogged down the shoulder past the donkey, who had stopped to nibble on some wildflowers. The big truck coming might work to my advantage, but I needed to get situated before it got up to us. I was sweating freely now, and my nice purple shirt was soaked. I got into position just as the truck arrived. It was moving slowly, maybe twenty miles an hour, and created a loud, scary wall to the left. I ran towards the donkey, waving my arms and the rope and shouting aggressively, trying to make the dirt road seem like the safest place to be.

The donkey bolted away from me, and I followed as fast as I could. The truck was passing the dirt road, so I only had a few seconds to use it. As the donkey got to the end of the fence, I went wide and threw the coiled rope out past it, holding on to one end. The donkey shied away from the rope and turned down the dirt road. I whipped the rope into the air and gave chase. If it doubled back on me now, I'd be in a mess, so I wanted to take that option completely off the table.

I don't know what possessed him to do it, but the truck driver honked his air horn as we rounded the corner. The blast of sound made me jump, but more importantly, it made the donkey take off like a shot. It flew down the road, leaving me far behind. It passed Erica and the deputy a minute later, and caught up with the mini. Together, they ran another hundred yards down the road and disappeared into a driveway on the left. I ran to catch up with them, but Erica was already closing the gate when I arrived, panting.

"Well, that was exciting," I said, leaning on the gate. "I hope this is where they live. If not, someone's going to be surprised when they get home."

The deputy chuckled. "It looked like they knew where they were going."

Erica pointed at the ground on the other side of the gate. "There's a bunch of hoof prints and mini horse poop in there, so this is it."

The driveway led to a small white house with a swing set and a red wagon in front of it. There was a telltale cardboard box sitting on the porch, further evidence supporting my hunch about how all of this had happened. I doubted that the delivery driver had left the gate open on purpose, but a moment of carelessness like that could have ended up in a horrible crash, with people and animals hurt or dead.

The mini and the donkey appeared around the right side of the house, still trotting, and came back up to the gate like we were all long lost friends. They were both blowing and heaving, and I guessed that this was the most activity either of them had had in quite some time. The donkey stuck his nose over the top of the gate, and I rubbed his face, scratching around his ears. Suddenly he sneezed, coating my face and shirt in a fine spray of snot and bits of grass and half-chewed wildflowers. I took my glasses off so I could see.

"That's nice," Erica said. She was wiping bits of overspray off her arm. "The flowers kind of go with your shirt."

"Thanks." I gave her a grin. "Think they'll let us in the restaurant like this?"

"I guess we're going to find out."

The three of us turned and headed back towards the pavement. There was a time in my younger days when I would have been upset about all this, sure that the Universe was trying to stick it to me. But by this point, I knew that this was just how it was being married to Erica. Regardless of what we're doing, there's a good chance of adventure, and I'm probably going to get dirty. At least this time it wasn't blood or poop.

7

The People You Meet

I've met a lot of people by going to see their horse on an emergency vet visit with Erica. For some of them, I'm meeting them on a really bad day, and they're stressed out of their minds. For others, it's not a major event, and they're calm and collected. The interesting thing to me is that the emotional state of the person is not always an accurate reflection of the physical state of the horse. Some people are hysterical about minor injuries or illnesses. Other people are placid when their horse is in a life-and-death situation. You just can't reliably predict the severity of an emergency based on the owner's emotional state.

Erica and I were leaving a mild gas colic one Saturday

morning. The horse was still uncomfortable, but it had drugs and fluids on board, and Erica was confident that it would be fine in an hour or two. I had a strong suspicion we'd be going back to see it again though, as the owner had a very low tolerance for discomfort in her horse. I much preferred those over the people who didn't call us until their horse had been in trouble for three days.

We made it about a mile down the road before Erica's phone rang.

"I figured she was going to call us again, but this seems awfully soon," I said.

"It's a different number," Erica said, swiping the green button on her phone. "Hello, Dr. Lacher."

"Hi Dr. Lacher. My name's Tatum Hand. I'm not a client of yours yet, as we just moved here, but I have an emergency." I'd totally forgotten that we'd been listening to a podcast through Erica's phone on the way to the colic, and that the volume on the radio was turned way up so we could hear it. When the caller's voice came through the stereo, it nearly deafened us both. Erica fumbled for the volume knob on the dash as I jammed my finger on the steering wheel button, and between the two of us, we got it down to a bearable level.

"Okay, where are you located, and what's going on?"

"We're on 241, south of Newberry Road. I have a mini, and something's going on with his right rear leg. He's not bending it at all."

We had just passed 241, so I got in the left lane and prepared to turn around at the next opening in the median. This was going to be a stellar response time to an emergency.

"Okay," Erica said. "I'm going to send you a link to our new client form. If you can work on filling that out for me, we'll be there in just a few minutes. We're actually right around the corner."

"Wonderful!"

Erica jotted down the address, and I got us headed back to the east. Five minutes later, we pulled up to the gate, where a slender blonde woman in her forties was waiting for us.

"Holy crap," I muttered, pointing over to the right as the gate swung open. "What is that?"

Erica followed my finger. "That's a Highland cow. Actually, I think it's a bull. I'm not sure I've ever seen one in person before."

It wasn't the biggest cow I'd ever seen, not by a long shot, but it was by far the hairiest cow I'd ever seen. It was solid reddish-brown, with medium length horns, and bangs that covered his eyes and most of his face. Words like *fluffy* and *cute* were coming to mind as I stared at it, terms I didn't generally associate with cows over the age of three months. If it's possible for a grown cow to look adorable, this guy had nailed it.

I pulled through the gate and parked. It was like driving into a newly constructed petting zoo. The fences and run-in sheds were all brand new lumber, with shiny green gates and silver water troughs everywhere. I turned in a slow circle and just took it in. The Highland bull was sharing a pen with two mini donkeys and a handful of chickens. Next to them, two calves were eating out of a feed pan. They looked like normal beef cows, plain and uninteresting after the hairy Highlander.

On the other side of the driveway, two mini horses were in a small paddock munching on hay. Behind them, in a large paddock, a line of goats stood at the gate, bleating at us. They ranged from tiny kids to huge and hairy, and I thought my heart was going to jump out of my chest and run over to them. At the end of the line, an adorable little gray baby goat got bumped out of the way, and a black and white pig waddled into its place.

"Oh, my," I breathed, feeling like a little kid in a toy store. I didn't even see the blonde woman approach us until she introduced herself.

"Hi, I'm Tatum. I can't believe you got here so fast, thank you for coming!" She shook hands with Erica. Her face was glowing, and she seemed to radiate positive energy. I liked her immediately, though I couldn't have said if it was her genuine good nature, or her collection of critters that won me over.

"This place is amazing," I said. "I could hang out here all day!"

Tatum laughed. "Thank you! It's a work in progress. My husband's been building fences and sheds every weekend. We've got all the big stuff done, but it was a huge project."

"I can imagine," I said. "He did a good job, though. If I tried to do something like this, there wouldn't be a single straight line on the property!"

She laughed. "Me, too! That's not my thing."

Erica pointed to the mini horses across the driveway. "I'm guessing that's our pony with the leg?"

"Yes!" Tatum turned and led us across the driveway. "This is Wild Man and Surfer Girl. Wild Man is the bay, and he's the one with the leg."

The goats were shuffling positions at the gate as we walked by them, and I noticed a second pig in the lineup. Behind the greeting committee, more goats and chickens dotted the paddock, standing on tree stumps or munching on weeds.

"Just so you know, we have a goat vet," I said. "She's pretty fantastic."

"Oh, I'm a goat vet," Tatum said. "I work on just about everything except horses. I'm a terrible horse vet."

Erica's eyebrows shot up. "I thought I knew every vet in this region. How did you not make it on my radar? Especially if you see goats!"

Tatum opened the gate and let us into the paddock with the minis. "Oh, I don't practice here in Florida yet. I still work in California for two weeks on, and two weeks off. We just moved out here a few months ago."

"Ah, that explains it." Erica grabbed a halter from the gate post, and we walked over to Wild Man. He didn't move, and I decided the name must be more about his forelock than his demeanor. The massive ball of hair on his head stuck out in every direction, like a black starburst. I wasn't sure the halter would fit over his mane, but Erica slid it in place with ease and handed me the lead rope.

Wild Man stood docilely as Erica ran her hands over his legs and back. He was much more well-behaved than most of the minis I'd dealt with, but I wasn't sure if he was a low-key kind of guy or if he was in a lot of pain. His face didn't look like he was hurting, but the punk rock hair-do made it hard to be sure.

"Okay, I think I know what's going on," Erica said, standing up. "Justin, see if he'll back up a few steps."

I clucked and pushed him lightly, and he took a step back, and then another one. "Like so?"

Erica nodded. "That's good. Now walk him forward."

I set off across the paddock, and Wild Man walked gamely beside me, and even stepped up to a trot. We turned around at the fence and walked back.

"It was a locking stifle, wasn't it?" Tatum asked. Erica nodded, and Tatum buried her face in her hands. "Oh, this is so embarrassing! I can't believe I didn't think of that. I went straight to major injury."

Erica laughed. "Don't feel bad, you said you weren't a horse vet! I'm a terrible small animal vet, so I promise, I get it. When my cats do something weird, I have to ask for help. That's without even acknowledging our inability to be objective about our own animals!"

"I know, but this was really basic. You shouldn't have had to come out here just to back him up a step."

I raised my hand. "Would you all mind explaining to me what happened? What's a locking stifle?"

"You can take the halter off," Erica said. "Horses can sleep standing up because of a thing called a reciprocal apparatus. Basically, they have these tendons in the back leg that slide over the joints and lock the leg in the vertical position so it can't bend. Then they can sleep without having to focus on keeping their leg muscles engaged. Some breeds, like minis, have a problem where the tendons don't pop back into place and unlock the leg like they're supposed to. That's called a locking stifle."

"Ahh, and taking a step back puts everything back where it belongs." I hung the halter back on the gate post. "That makes sense."

"I knew about this, but I've never had to deal with it before," Tatum said. "We just got Wild Man about three weeks ago, and this is the first time he's done it since we've had him."

"It seems like the best possible thing that could go wrong with a horse," I said.

"For sure," Erica agreed.

We stepped back out the gate and stopped to admire the goats. One of them bore a strong resemblance to Wild Man, with a massive mane going in every direction. I had never wanted a goat as much as I did in that moment.

"It must have been a challenge to get everyone moved all the way across the country," I said. "How many trips did that take?"

"Oh, none of them came from California," Tatum said. "I went on a bit of a collecting spree last month. These are all new to us. I've been dreaming about having a hobby farm all my life, and now that I finally have one, I got a bit carried away."

"I think it's great!" I said.

Tatum smiled. "I think so too, but I've got a lot of work to do. There are about ten intact male goats to castrate, which I'm dreading, and one of the donkeys is intact, too."

"If you're interested in having some help, this would be a great opportunity for some vet students to get some hands-on experience," Erica said. "I can set that up with the vet school."

Tatum's face lit up. "Oh, that would be fantastic! I've been so apprehensive about doing this by myself. We can make a day of it and do a cookout for everyone. This will be a great experience for the students! Oh, my gosh, this is wonderful news!"

We nearly always have a student or two rotating through the clinic to get real-world veterinary experience. Erica loves teaching the next generation of doctors, and she's always on the lookout for opportunities like this. It really was a perfect situation. There were enough animals to give a group of ten students a chance to do something important, but relatively low risk, and since the owner was also a veterinarian, she wasn't going to be stressed out about students working on her animals.

"I'll get it set up," Erica said. "I can have three vets and three techs here, and maybe a dozen students. We've got a mobile surgery center in an RV, so we can bring that out. That way we can teach them how to do a castration in the field, and how it goes in a hospital setting."

"Wow, you guys have a mobile hospital?"

"We're working on building a small animal clinic onto our equine clinic," I explained. "Now that we've got a mixed animal vet, we need the proper facilities to do that stuff. We bought the RV to tide us over until the construction is done. It has a wet table and a surgery table, everything you need. It's a pretty sweet setup."

"I'm really impressed with you all," Tatum said. "I mean, I was impressed with your facility when I was looking at your website earlier, but this is even more exciting! If you're building a small animal hospital, then you're probably going to add another small animal vet at some point, right?"

Erica and I exchanged a glance. We had been talking about this expansion for over a year, and one of the scariest things we were up against was finding a second doctor to help make the additional space pay for itself. Veterinarians were in short supply across the nation, a problem that was getting worse every year. Here we were, at an emergency on a Saturday morning, and a small animal vet was falling into our laps. Were we dreaming?

"If you're looking to stop commuting from Florida to California, we would definitely be interested in talking to you about that," I said.

Tatum nodded vigorously. "I'm not in a rush to quit, so our timelines probably align well. But I do have two weeks of free time every month, if you want some help. I do exotic animals too, if you have any of those around. I used to be a movie set vet in Hollywood, so I've worked with all kinds of birds, bears, big cats, everything. I have a dart gun and a pole syringe, too. I can do whatever you need me to do. Except horses, obviously!"

We all shared a laugh at that.

"We would love to have you on the team," Erica said. "We actually do have one circus client. I don't suppose you know much about chickens, do you? We get calls about chickens more frequently than I ever would have expected."

"I actually did a surgery on a chicken three days ago," Tatum said. "Chicken people are very committed to taking care of their animals. I deal with a lot of bumblefoot, egg-bound hens, animal attacks, that kind of stuff."

"You're hired!" Erica said. "None of us know anything about chickens. Dr. Hanks actually sewed one up that had been attacked by a fox a while back, but she really doesn't want to be a chicken vet."

Erica and Tatum talked shop for a few more minutes, and I squatted down by the gate to pet the goats. Some of them shied away, but most of them climbed over each other to try and get some scratches. The one with the giant spiked mane fluff worked his way to the front and bleated at me. I ruffled his impressive hair, then took a picture of him. He looked perpetually surprised and excited, a combination that tickled me to no end. Now that I had experienced that level of goat cuteness, would my life ever be the same?

At last, we said our goodbyes and made our way back down the driveway. The hairy Highlander watched us go, his stillness accentuated by the goat activity across the yard. This had been an unusual emergency, to say the least. Not only had it been filled with cute critters, but we also had a wet lab set up for some vet students, and a new doctor ready to become part of our team.

"Well," I said, pulling out onto the highway. "That's not how I thought today was going to go."

Erica chuckled. "Right? I mean, who expects to go to an emergency and hire a new vet instead?"

"The Wendy's commercials have been telling us all our lives: *if you build it, they will come*. Looks like they were right all along."

"I guess so."

I was filled with optimism about the future. Dr. Hand was a fountain of enthusiasm, and I knew she would be a great addition to our team. Things were coming together in very unexpected ways, and it was yet another reminder for me to trust the work that Erica and I were doing. As long as we stayed true to our mission to make the world a better place for horses (and all the other animals, too!) and continued to work towards that, the right people would be drawn to us. The proof was in the pudding.

8

Big Things in Little Packages

It was a beautiful Saturday morning in April. I had just finished my monthly appearance on *The Love and Victory Show*, a weekly live radio and YouTube program on which I'd managed to land a regular guest spot. I was packing the lights and camera away when Erica poked her head in the door.

"All clear?" she asked.

I nodded. "Yep, it finished on time today. But you seem to be done riding a little early."

"That's because we have an emergency."

"Well, poop," I said.

"Actually, no poop," Erica said. "That's the problem. It's

a new mini foal, and it looks like it's constipated."

I put the video camera back in the case, and decided the rest of the gear could wait. "I just need to change clothes quick," I said. "Are we taking the vet student?"

"Yep. I need to change quick, too, and I told Sarah we'd pick her up in five minutes."

Sarah was a vet student at Auburn, and would be a doctor at the end of May. She was spending a two-month rotation at our clinic to be mentored by Erica, and we tried to take her on all the emergencies we could to get her more hands-on experience. It was convenient that she was staying at a neighbor's house, as we could pick her up on the way by without losing any time.

Ten minutes later, the three of us were cruising down the highway towards High Springs. Sarah was in the back seat pouring over a textbook on foal care that Erica had loaned her, trying to come up with a list of possible complications based on the information that we had so far.

"Do we know exactly when the foal was born?" Sarah asked.

"Not precisely," Erica said. "Sometime Thursday night or early Friday morning."

"Did we pull an IgG on it yesterday?"

"No, the owner doesn't do any vet care outside of emergencies."

"Huh," Sarah grunted. "You said this is a mini breeding operation, right?"

Erica nodded. "Yeah, but it's a low-budget breeding operation. She does a pretty good job managing things, but we don't do any uterine cultures, ultrasounds, vaccines, none of that stuff. And no IgG tests."

"Okay, so we don't know if the foal got sufficient colostrum yesterday," Sarah said, jotting down some notes. "Do we know if it's been nursing?"

"Owner says he's nursing just fine and has plenty of energy, but when he does the tail up and leg spread to poop, nothing's coming out. He'll try a few times, then give up."

"Do we know if he passed the meconium?"

"Unknown."

Sarah was silent for a minute as she flipped pages in the textbook. I was deeply absorbed in the conversation, as this sort of assessment normally happened inside Erica's head. The process was surprisingly similar to troubleshooting a computer problem, which put it in a context I could grasp.

Is there power?

Yes.

Proceed to item 4.

Does Windows load normally?

No.

Proceed to item 12.

"It looks like we need to do a physical exam before we can make any guesses," Sarah said. "Everything depends on temp and heart rate as to whether we're dealing with a virus, bacterial infection, or just constipation."

"Okay," Erica said. "What's our heart rate range?"

"Sixty to one hundred for a foal," Sarah said. "Wait, this is a mini foal, does that change our numbers?"

"It might change them a bit, but not dramatically. But you do have to consider that on everything you do with a mini, especially dosing drugs. It's hard to get an accurate weight on them without a scale, and there's so much variety in the size and shape of minis that there's not an exact number for a lot of this stuff. So on heart rate, if it was one hundred and twenty, I'd still be okay with that, unless something else was giving me an indication of a problem. It's all subjective."

We passed through High Springs and turned north toward Fort White. The countryside was covered in small farms and horses. As we crossed over the Santa Fe River, flashes of red and yellow kayaks passing beneath the bridge caught my eye. This was a very popular river, as it was lined with huge natural springs of clear water gushing up out of the ground. A few minutes later, we pulled into a tree-covered driveway.

"Oh, this place is cute!" Sarah said. "Everything's tiny!"

The driveway was flanked by paddocks. Huge sprawling live oak trees shaded much of the area, and each side had a low run-in shed that would be way too short for a regular horse, but was perfect for a mini. There were two very pregnant mares on each side, seemingly as round as they were long. Dana, the owner, was waiting at the gate, and opened it as we approached.

Erica pointed to the right side of the yard as we entered. "There they are, over by the shed. Go ahead and stop here."

A brown and white miniature mare stood eating out of a bucket, the lead rope from her halter draped over her shoulders. She was remarkably fit for a mini, especially one that had just given birth a few days prior. I remembered from previous trips out here that Dana kept all of her minis in good shape, which is hard to do. A tiny tan foal was running circles around her.

"Good morning," Erica called as she opened her door. I hastily climbed out and met them at the back of the vet truck and opened the hatchback.

"Good morning," Dana said. "Thanks for coming out. Sorry to call you on a Saturday."

"No worries," Erica said. "This is almost-doctor Sarah, she's doing a clinical rotation with us before she graduates from vet school next month."

"Nice to meet you," Sarah said, extending her hand. "Your place is adorable!"

"Thanks," Dana said, shaking her hand. "Sometimes I wish I'd just gotten into crocheting or something. These babies are making me old before my time."

"I bet," Sarah said with a laugh. "Let's see what's going on with this little guy." She put a few things in the tray from the vet box and handed it to me.

We walked across the yard, and Dana grabbed the lead rope from the mare's back. "One advantage to minis is that you can ground tie them with food," she said. "I just put some hay in a little net and put it in the bucket, and you couldn't drag her away."

The foal was a different story. His mom might not be moving, but he was like an erratic pinball. His movements were twitchy, as all foals started out, which made him hard to predict. As he circled around the back of his mom, I stepped in to grab him. His head twitched to the left, which made me think he was turning that way, and I lunged to mirror his movement. As it turned out, it was an unintentional jerk rather than a tell move, and as I moved to his left, he went right and easily trotted past me. Fortunately, Erica was ready for him, and slid a hand around his neck.

"He faked me out," I said, dropping to my knees to hold the foal for the exam. "Can you tell I never played football?"

"Not at all," Erica said as she stepped back. "Okay Sarah, he's all yours."

This was the tiniest foal I'd ever held, and it was awkward. For most foals, I rest their neck in the crook of my elbow and use that hand to keep their head from swinging around. This fellow was more like holding a long-legged goat, and my arms were blocking Sarah from doing anything. I scooted back and cupped his chin with one hand, and held his butt straight with my other hand. That was much better, at least while she was listening to his heart and gut sounds.

"Okay, heart rate is about ninety," Sarah said. "Lots of gut sounds on this side. Let's get a temp."

I slid my hand down his flanks so Sarah could raise his tail and insert the thermometer. As soon as she did, it turned into a rodeo. His butt launched straight up in the air, and he kicked out sideways, nailing me right in the ribs. He was too small for it to hurt much, but I didn't have time to think about pain anyway. While his back end was bucking, his front end was trying to take off. He managed to twist his head out of my hand, so I grabbed him around the chest instead. I was on my knees, so I couldn't really go anywhere. He stomped on my thighs about fifteen times in two seconds before I could get him straightened out and squeezed up against my chest. His mom rolled an eye in our direction, but her muzzle never left the bucket of hay.

"Well, that was exciting," I grunted. The foal squirmed in my arms, and suddenly tossed his head, clocking me right in the jaw. That was enough to make me not want another hit, and I clamped his head up against my chest. "Do it while I've got him."

Sarah made a second effort to get his temperature. This

time, there was nowhere to go, and he didn't struggle much. "101," she announced. "Can you turn him around?"

It took a few tries to get his head going in the right direction, but I managed to get the foal turned around and standing still so she could listen to his abdomen on the other side. After a moment, she stepped back and motioned Erica forward.

"Do you want to take a listen?"

"Sure," Erica said, popping her stethoscope in her ears. She slid the diaphragm around a few different places, then stepped back. "Okay, you can let him run around a minute."

I released him, and he sprinted in a circle around his mom, then stopped to nurse.

"His heart rate and temp are normal," Erica said, turning to Dana. "Have you seen him successfully poop at all?"

Dana shook her head. "No, he lifts his tail up and spreads his legs, and you can tell he's pushing, but nothing happens."

As if on cue, the foal stopped nursing and took a step back. He widened his stance and grew very still as his tail raised straight up in the air. His eyes were focused on some distant point, as if he were trying desperately hard to read a sign across the street. His whole body trembled briefly, and suddenly it was over. He dropped his tail and wandered around to sniff at the hay his mother was eating.

"Let's put the ultrasound on him and take a quick look," Erica said.

She pulled her phone out of her pocket and Sarah handed her the probe from the tray. Erica plugged the probe into her phone and opened the program.

"You can do an ultrasound with your phone?" Dana's eyebrows shot up.

"Yeah, it's pretty fantastic," Erica said. "It doesn't work for everything, but it's great for colics."

"It definitely beats standing here holding the big ultrasound machine," I said. "That thing weighs a ton."

The foal wandered over, and I snagged him before he could walk away. I got back down on my knees, mindful of how he had pummeled me the first time around, and squeezed him up against my chest as Erica handed the probe to Sarah.

"I'm going to get alcohol on your legs," Sarah said.

I nodded. "Go ahead, I'll manage. I'd rather get wet than get stomped again."

She giggled, then squirted alcohol all over his side so the ultrasound would be able to see through his hair. It ran down his ribs and dripped off onto my shorts. It was cold and unpleasant for both of us, and I apologized to the foal as we struggled to deal with the situation.

"Sorry, kiddo. Just hang tight, we're going to get through this together."

Erica watched the screen over Sarah's shoulder and corrected the angle of the probe as she pressed it against his abdomen. "You always want to be conscious of your angle to the body wall. Keep your vertical position so you know which way is up, and slide it down and try to stay at ninety degrees as you follow the curve. There you go, nice and slow."

"Is that small intestine?" Sarah asked. "Right beside the rib?"

I glanced at the screen. Small intestine was about the only thing I could recognize on an ultrasound, and only because I'd watched Erica do it on a hundred colics over the years. While most of the screen looked like static, small intestine looked like a stack of black bubbles with a white outline. It was much harder for me to see from a distance on the phone screen than on the big ultrasound, but I recognized the shape just as Erica confirmed it.

"Yep, that's right. Now, if you go up and move it back just a bit, we should be able to see enough of it to tell if things are moving."

Sarah squirted more alcohol on the foal, soaking my lap in the process. Erica guided Sarah's hand with the probe, and they looked at a few more areas before finishing the exam. The foal and I suffered through it with minimal struggling, seemingly equally resigned to our fates for the moment.

"It looks like a meconium impaction," Erica said at last, standing upright. "That's good news. It's the easiest thing to treat out of all the things that could have been wrong with him. I'll pull some blood so we can run a panel and rule out some things when we get back to the clinic, but we're going to treat him with an enema and see if that solves his problems."

"Okay," Dana said. "Sounds good."

I released the foal again, and we headed back to the truck to get supplies. My shorts were soaked with alcohol and plastered to my leg like I'd had a bathroom accident, and my shirt was wet and covered in foal hair, but I doubted that the worst of it had happened yet. I grabbed the bucket and squirted some dish soap in it.

"Let's put some more in there," Erica said, stopping me as I was putting the soap away. "This is a rare occasion when more is better." I added another long squirt to the bucket, and she nodded. "Perfect. Half full of water should be plenty."

I stepped back as she opened the bottom drawer and

selected a small rubber tube. She put it in the bucket, then grabbed the lube bottle and the dose syringe and handed them to Sarah.

"This is going to get messy," Erica said. "Justin will hold him, and you're going to insert the tube rectally. I'll tell you when to stop. You want to be super gentle, because it's easy to accidentally have a rectal tear, and that's really bad. We'll use lots of lube and go slow, and if you feel resistance, don't force it. Once we're in, I'll fill the dose syringe for you, and you'll administer it."

"Okay." Sarah sounded more confident than she looked, but this was a good thing to be nervous about. A rectal tear would probably mean the end of the road for the foal, and more than a few horse owners have killed their foal trying to do an enema themselves. It seemed like a straightforward task, but inserting the tube walked a fine line between saving the horse and killing it.

The foal was nursing when we got back, so we waited a minute for it to finish. I grabbed him just as he unlatched, and we shuffled over away from the mare a few feet. His ribs were soaked in alcohol, but he seemed to have given up on struggling. I expected that to change the instant the tube went in his butt. Dana walked around to get a better view of the action, and I shook my head.

"You don't want to stand in the backblast area," I warned her. "Anything within ten feet of him on that end is about to be the danger zone."

I could practically see the gears falling into place in her head as her eyes widened. "Oh. Oh! Good call, I'll just stand over here in the safe zone."

Sarah coated the end of the tube with lubricant and

moved over beside me. Erica took her place opposite Sarah, and they got right to work.

"It's a lot like passing an NG tube up the nose," Erica said. "You're doing everything by feel. You'll know if something feels different, like you're hitting resistance. As soon as that happens, you stop and back up a bit. Twist the tube as you go, and that will help it follow the path of least resistance."

I held the foal's tail up with one hand, and tightened my grip on his chest with the other. I had my arm all the way around his neck this time, since all the work was happening on the back end. As expected, he attempted to shoot off like a rocket as soon as Sarah inserted the tube. I was braced for it and managed to keep him mostly in place. Once the initial struggle subsided, she continued.

"Hold steady, little buddy," I said, whispering into his ear as it brushed my face. "Nobody likes this part, but you're going to feel better when it's over."

He flicked his ear at me but stood still once more. I felt bad for him. His second day in the world wasn't going great. He needed to poop and couldn't, he was soaked with alcohol, and now he had a tube going in places he definitely didn't want it. It was a rough welcome.

"Okay, that's good," Erica said. "Let's give him some fluid and see what happens."

She handed Sarah the dose syringe. It was filled with soapy water, and looked like a giant kid's toy version of a needle and syringe. Sarah stuck the tube on the tip of it, braced the handle on her hip, and began slowly pushing water through it.

"How fast should I go?" she asked.

"About like that," Erica said. "You don't want to blast it in."

The foal went rigid in my arms. A second later, a stream of orange water shot past the tube and out of his butt, spraying out all over the place.

"Pull the tube out, quick!" Erica stepped back, but not fast enough to avoid the spackle of water that coated her leg. Sarah hadn't moved, and the rust-colored glob of poop that followed the tube out landed right on her boot. Once that was out, orange water sprayed out like a fountain, going six feet in every direction. I could feel it coating my hand as I held his tail, but there was nothing I could do about it.

When the flow died down to a trickle, Erica came back over. "Okay, let's do it again."

Sarah looked at her hand and the tube, which were now the color of pumpkin pie. "Should I wash up first?"

Erica laughed. "No, it won't help. The inside is the same way, now. Let's just get some more water in him."

Erica squirted some lubricant on the tube, since her hands were still clean, and Sarah repeated the process. Now that the meconium block was out of the way, the water went in easier. She put in about half the water from the dose syringe before Erica stopped her.

"Okay, let's see what we've got."

Sarah pulled the tube out, and orange water shot out in a straight line, easily traveling ten feet. A few bits of mushy poop came out as well, and then a few more. I could feel the foal's gut contracting as he pushed, and the second effort sprayed out in all directions again, coating Sarah in a fine mist.

I glanced over at Dana and grinned. "See what I mean? He's got an impressive range for a little guy."

Dana covered her laugh with a hand. “It went a lot further than I would have thought possible. Should I get her a towel or something?”

I glanced at Sarah. The right side of her face was freckled with orange spots, and the sunlight reflected off the drops hanging on a few loose hairs in her bangs. Her shirt and pants were similarly adorned, and the hand holding the tube was orange up to her elbow. I started to mention that the meconium glob was still on her boot, but decided there wasn't any point.

“I think we may have to hit her with the water hose and tie her to the roof rack for the ride home,” I said. “But she could probably use a towel, if you have an old one you can sacrifice.”

“I breed horses,” Dana said with a laugh. “All of my towels get sacrificed.”

“Is it normal for it to smell this bad?” Sarah asked. “I mean, I know it's poop, but it's really rank.”

“Welcome to foals,” Erica said. “Milk poop is foul. Meconium is even worse, because it's like thick grease, and you can't get it off your shoe if you step in it.”

We all glanced down at Sarah's boot as she lifted it gingerly into the air. “Great. Why did I want to be a vet again?”

“Because we get to play with baby horses!” Erica said. “This is just like the brochure, right? Be a vet, play with cute babies all day!”

The foal strained in my arms again, and a little more runny poop dribbled out. “Can I let him go?” I asked.

Erica shook her head. “Not quite. I think he's okay now, we just need to grab some blood and clean his little bum so he doesn't get a rash.”

I adjusted my grip so Erica could get to his neck, and she quickly pulled a few cc's of blood. Sarah used the dose syringe to spray water on the back of his legs, tail, and my orange hand, and Erica toweled him off. I let him go and slowly climbed to my feet, my back protesting every move.

The foal was clearly feeling better about things. He ran in circles around his mom, who still had her head buried in the bucket eating hay. Every third or fourth stride was accompanied by a buck, and his little back feet kicked out to the side. He let out a shrill whinny, and I couldn't help but laugh. It looked like his bad day had turned around.

Dana brought out a stack of towels, and we spent some time at the water hose trying to get clean enough to get inside the vet truck. Sarah had definitely gotten the worst of it, but Erica had her share of it, too. I might have gotten the worse end of the alcohol part during the ultrasound, but I had fared pretty well on the poop spackling, except for the hand that had held his tail. I considered it a good trade.

Sarah and I cleaned the gear while Erica typed up the bill. The smell made me want to puke, which I used as motivation to get it clean as fast as possible. The chlorhexidine didn't have much of an odor, which was normally how I would have preferred it, but just this once, a little bit of a disinfectant smell might have been a good thing. Sarah spent a few minutes trying to get her boot clean, and then we hauled everything to the truck and put it away.

On the ride home, Erica and Sarah talked about the case. I only listened with half an ear, as the excitement was pretty much over at that point. I was glad that Sarah had been able to experience this one with us. Even if there was a lot of disgusting poop spray involved, it had been a great teaching opportunity for her, and we got to play with a very cute baby. There's almost always a silver lining. Sometimes you just have to look past the poop to see it.

9

Managing Madness

One Sunday morning, Erica was out back riding her horse, which is how she tempts fate when she's on call. To be fair, she can be back in the barn, unsaddled, and upstairs to change clothes in less than five minutes. I was at the computer, editing the latest podcast recording. I had Google Voice open on my second screen, just so I would have a heads up if an emergency happened.

We use Google Voice for our emergency hotline. That allows us to transfer the number to whichever doctor is on call. It also allows me to see the transcripts of the voicemails people leave, which is often entertaining. Not because of the emergencies, mind you, but because the transcript software doesn't always do a very good job. The message that popped up on my screen took me a minute to decipher.

This is Monica caution. I just got hit by an archer. I think the house is are fine but the doors are cursed. I need help. Please call me back.

Archer is the name of the next town south of us, and also the name of the road between Archer and Gainesville. That part was fairly easy to figure out, but the rest of it left me scratching my head. I stepped out on the porch to see if Erica had gotten the message yet. She was riding up to the barn, already on the phone.

"Is it safe to drive?" Erica asked. She was on her Bluetooth headset, so I couldn't hear the other side of the conversation. "Okay, I think the best answer is to go back to your house and we'll work on getting them out there. That way we don't have to figure out another trailer to get them home."

We were clearly going to see whatever this was, so I went back in and closed the podcast I'd been working on. By the time I filled my water bottle and grabbed a granola bar, Erica was upstairs.

"What do we have?" I asked, following her to the bedroom.

"Trailer wreck. Not a bad one, but the trailer doors are caved in, so we're going to have to figure out how to get them open so we can get the horses off."

"Ah, she got hit by Archer," I said. "I was trying to decipher Google's transcription. Who is it?"

"Monica Cauthon. She's on Archer Road."

"Oh, I know her. And she thinks the horses are fine. Got it."

Erica pulled a light green scrub top over her head and tucked it into her pants. "She texted me a picture of the trailer. I think we can probably cut it open with the Sawzall."

I grabbed her phone off the bed and opened the text. The trailer doors were indeed crushed in, and the vertical bar with the camlocks that locked them in the closed position were bent in at the top and bottom at a 45° angle. The top camlock was still latched, but the bottom one was nearly a foot inside the trailer, wedged into the floor. There was a one-foot gap between the doors, just enough to see that there was a horse inside.

"Alright, let me get some tools," I said. "We might be able to take the hinges apart, but we may have to cut that bar. That's going to make a ton of noise and probably freak out the horses, so that will be a last resort. How many horses are on the trailer?"

"Two. And they're pretty good most of the time."

"Well, they just got the back of their trailer caved in, so I wouldn't blame them for being panicky. She lives on the south side of Paynes Prairie, right?" I grabbed my water bottle off the counter as we went out the door.

"Right. But she has to wrap things up with the police before she can leave the scene, so we're not racing to get there."

I stopped at my toolbox down in the feed room and gathered everything I thought I might need to get the doors off the trailer. Sawzall, prybars, screwdrivers, grinder, and a handful of wrenches. We loaded it all in the backseat of the vet truck and took off down the driveway.

It was a thirty-five-minute drive to Monica's house, according to Google Maps. About fifteen minutes into the trip, Erica's phone rang again. I turned down the music.

"Hello, Dr. Lacher."

"Just hold the dang horse, Emily! I'm calling the vet right now." The woman's voice coming over the speakers was unfamiliar, but I recognized the tone of stress that mothers get when dealing with an exasperating child.

"Hello, this is Dr. Lacher," Erica repeated. "Can you hear me?"

"Yes, sorry about that. This is Jennifer King."

"Oh, hi, Jennifer. What's going on?"

"We were bringing the horses in to saddle up a few minutes ago. Emily was walking Snooter across the asphalt part of the driveway, and the neighbor started his mower, and it backfired. And you know Snooter, he's flighty, so he spooked hard, and slipped on the asphalt and went down pretty hard. He's skinned up in a few spots, and he's limping a little bit, but I don't know if you need to come see him or not."

"Mom, he's bleeding, she needs to come!" The teenage girl in the background wasn't near as calm as her mother.

"Let's start with some pictures of all the scrapes and bloody spots," Erica said. "Then if you want to walk him around in a figure eight and video that, I can take a look at how he's moving. You can send those to me on the emergency number. But if he's not overtly lame, my guess is that he's just a bit sore from the fall, and that will go away in a day or two."

"Okay, we can do that," Jennifer said. "I'll send you some pictures right now."

"Sounds good," Erica said. "I'll call you back as soon as I get a look at them, and we'll make a plan."

I turned left onto Archer Road as they hung up. "Where do they live?" I asked.

"The other direction, unfortunately," Erica said, opening her computer. "She's between Alachua and High Springs."

"Oh boy. Hopefully it's not bad." We were still fifteen minutes away from Monica's, plus the time it would take to get the horse trailer opened. "At least we can take the interstate up from here. That will be a little faster, if we have to go, but we're probably two hours away at best."

Erica's phone dinged as the pictures began arriving. Before she could even scroll through them, it began ringing again. She waited for the number to pop up before answering.

"Is that Jennifer again?" I asked, hoping for the best.

Erica shook her head. "Nope, different number. Hello, this is Dr. Lacher."

The voice that filled the truck was that of an old man trying not to cry and losing the battle. "Dr. Lacher, this is Edward Stanton." He took a shaky breath and cleared his throat. "Old Milton is down out in the back pasture. I've been trying to get him up, but he just ain't wanting to do it."

I remained silent as I navigated the lights and traffic around the interstate exchange, but inside I was starting to panic. The emergencies were piling up on us faster than Erica could even manage the phone calls. As usual, she was calm and controlled as she answered him.

"Oh, no," she said. "Do you know how long he's been down?"

"I reckon he's been there a good part of the night," Edward said. His voice was rough, like someone was shaking a can of wet gravel. "He's got the ground tore up a bit, like he was trying to get up, but he ain't tried since I came out to find him this morning. It ain't like him to skip breakfast."

"No, he's definitely food-motivated," Erica agreed,

tapping the keys on her computer. "It looks like he's twenty-nine now, is that right?"

"Carol bought him in 1997," Edward said. "I told her she didn't have no business trying to train a three-year-old at her age. She was sixty-four then, you know, but she didn't pay me no mind. So I guess he'd be twenty-nine now."

"Carol always did what she wanted to do," Erica said with a chuckle. "You were just there to make sure it all happened the way she wanted it."

"She had her own plans for things." Edward managed a chuckle. "She had Milton driving a cart in two years, and they won their first marathon two years after that. I'm glad she's not here to see him down like this, it'd tear her up inside."

"I'm about to pull up to another emergency right now," Erica said. "It's a minor trailer wreck, but I don't know how long it's going to take me. If Milton is safe where he is, I'd just let him be still for now. It's cloudy today, so that's a good thing. You might bring a bucket of water out where he can reach it, and some hay for him to munch on, just to try and make him as comfortable as possible. I'll give you a call when we get done here, and we'll go from there. Okay?"

"I'll get him took care of," Edward said. "Carol would have me build him a shade canopy, I expect. I'll keep him in hay and water until you get out here."

We were pulling into Monica's neighborhood as Erica hung up the phone. Ahead of us, an empty rollback tow truck was pulling into her driveway. "Looks like she called in reinforcements," I said. "That'll make this a whole lot easier."

I pulled in behind the tow truck and followed him around the curve to the barn.

"Looks like we beat her," Erica said. "Did we pass her

somewhere? I didn't see a trailer on the side of the road anywhere."

"Not that I saw," I said, pulling into a shady spot and turning off the truck. "But I don't know where it happened."

"Me either," Erica said. "Somewhere on Archer Road."

"Don't forget about Snooter," I said.

"Snooter," Erica said, picking her phone back up. "I need to look at Snooter pics."

While she checked the messages from Jennifer, I got out and walked over to the tow truck. A stocky black man of about thirty-five climbed down out of the cab. His finely trimmed beard, along with the blue polo shirt and slacks he was wearing, clashed with my expectations. He grinned broadly and stuck out his hand.

"Man, am I glad to see you guys!" He laughed heartily as he shook my hand. "I thought I was being sent out here to do some kind of crazy horse rescue all by myself."

"You? I thought I was going to have to try to cut these trailer doors open all by *my*self. I can't tell you how relieved I am to have a pro on the scene!"

"Well, I guess it's a lucky day for both of us," he said. "I'm Shawn, by the way. Is that Dr. Lacher over there?"

"It is," I said. "I'm Justin. I'm the night and weekend emergency tech."

"Oh, you're the husband I hear about," he said with a grin. "I've got a couple of horses, and Dr. Lacher's my vet. If she's here, I know we're going to be fine. That lady is the Boss."

"For sure," I agreed. "She's the MacGyver of the horse world."

He stared at me for a long moment, squinting, his head

tilted slightly to the right. "I know you," he said at last, his face lighting up in a grin. "Yeah. You're the Horse Girl, right? From the videos? I saw you on Facebook. Man, you crack me up with the belly button ring and everything!"

I had to laugh. Along with being married to the most famous equine vet there is, I've also written eight books, I host one of the biggest equine podcasts in the world, and I've produced dozens and dozens of horse healthcare videos, but my role as Horse Girl in our tongue-in-cheek comedy video series on YouTube was the thing that was going to put me on the map. It might not have been my first choice for stardom, but if that was what got me my ten minutes of fame, I'd take it.

"That's me," I said. "I gotta say, I never thought I'd be shopping for belly button rings on Amazon when I was forty-seven, but that's been one of the most fun projects we've done."

He let out another deep belly laugh. "You're committed, man. I don't think I could pierce something just for a video!"

"Oh, I didn't get it pierced," I said. "It's just a clip-on thing. But it looks good, right?"

"It looked real to me!"

We both turned at the sound of a horse trailer rattling out on the street. A big white SUV was pulling in the driveway, and another one was right behind it pulling a two-horse slant load trailer. I turned back to let Erica know they had arrived, but she was already walking across the grass to join us.

"How were the Snooter pictures?" I asked.

"He's fine, just a little scraped up. We don't have to go see him at the moment." She leaned over and looked past me. "Hey Shawn, what are you doing here? I thought you drove a school bus."

"Hey, Dr. Lacher! Good to see you. This is my other job. The school bus thing just pays for the horses."

"Well, you make it look good," she said. "That's the best tow truck uniform I've ever seen."

Shawn laughed. "I was on my way to church when the dispatcher called me. I've got a pair of coveralls if I need them."

"Hopefully it won't come to that," Erica said, stepping over to the driveway as the SUV with the trailer pulled to a stop in front of the barn. "Let's see what we've got."

Monica got out of the driver's side, a small, handsome woman in her mid-fifties with short dirty-blonde hair. Her daughter got out the other side and walked around to join us. She was around thirty, and a spitting image of her mother. We moved back to the trailer, where Erica climbed up on the running board and peered in the open window.

"I couldn't see any injuries," Monica said. "I was stopped at the light, and the F-250 behind me just ran right into us. I'm sure the horses got banged around in their slots, but I don't think either of them went down."

"Okay, that's good. I don't see anything obvious, but let's get the trailer opened up so we can get a good look at them." She stepped back down and walked behind the trailer.

The pictures Monica sent had represented the situation well. Both doors were pushed in, and the vertical locking rods were bent in and jammed into the floor, preventing the doors from coming back out. The horse in the back slot let out a deafening whinny and stomped the floor a few times.

"They know they're home," Monica said. "They're

probably never going to get on a trailer again after this."

"Oh, you'd be surprised how well they handle stuff like this," Erica said. "I'm going to grab some sedation and see if I can get it into them through the windows. The last thing we need is for them to lose it now while we're trying to get the doors open."

While she ran back to the vet truck, Shawn and I started working out a plan.

"I was thinking we could cut this rod with a Sawzall," I said. "That's going to make a ton of noise though, and I don't know if that's a good idea with the horses in there. Do you have a better idea?"

"I can probably just pull them open with the winch," he said. "That might do a lot more damage to the trailer, though."

I glanced down at the hinge on the right side. The aluminum was already torn across the top. "We could try that, but I'd worry about it ripping the hinge off and still being stuck in the middle. It's hard to guess how much pressure is on that rod."

Shawn nodded in agreement. "Yeah, we don't want to make it unrepairable if we don't have to." He stepped up on the exposed ledge and examined the camlocks at the top. "It looks like there's just these two bolts holding this whole locking plate on. We might be able to pull those and remove the whole locking assembly."

"That would be ideal," I said. "If we can do this without power tools, that's our best bet. I didn't bring any Allen wrenches though, did you?"

"Yeah, I've got a socket set with Allens. I'll back the truck up against the trailer here so I've got something to stand on."

He jogged over to the tow truck, and I glanced around the corner of the trailer. Erica was halfway in the front window, her toes barely touching the running board. A moment later she popped out, her face flushed.

"Okay, all set," she said. "Did you guys come up with a plan?"

I nodded. "I think so. Hopefully we can just pull a couple of bolts and do this without spooking the horses with a bunch of racket."

Once the tow truck was in position, Shawn used the hydraulics to slide the bed back right up against the trailer. He grabbed a toolbox and climbed up, and the rest of us gathered around to watch.

Even with the long ratchet handle for leverage, the bolt was tight. Shawn was a muscular guy, and he was putting some effort into this. Again, I was glad that Monica had called him, because I wouldn't have had the right tools to do this, and it would have been a difficult job for me at best, and I might not have been able to do it at all.

The bolt slowly grew longer as Shawn backed it out. Without warning, it shot out with a loud bang, pulling the ratchet out of his hand and sending it skidding across the truck bed as the right-side door slammed into the bed of the tow truck. We all jumped, including the horses. Even sedated, they didn't like explosions happening at the back of the trailer, and who could blame them?

"Well, that was under some pressure, huh?" I said with a nervous chuckle. "Shawn, are you okay?"

He shook his head. "Man, I'm glad I didn't get shot with that bolt. It went right by my elbow."

"I'm glad you backed the truck up to it," I said. "Imagine

if you'd been standing on the back of the trailer! That would have been at head level."

He shivered. "Everything about horses is dangerous, man, even things you don't think about." He stepped over and picked up the ratchet. "One down, one to go. I'll be ready for this one, though."

Standing to the side, he began removing the bolt holding the other end of the plate to the trailer frame. Now that we knew how much pressure was on the vertical rod, we all stepped back a few feet. I tried to imagine what would have happened if I'd cut the rods with the Sawzall. I would have been standing on the back of the trailer, or maybe on a ladder or mounting block. It likely would have broken the blade when it popped, which would have been right at eye level for me, and the door would have slammed into me, probably followed by a terrified horse. There was no way it could have worked out well.

"Here we go," Shawn said, moving as far to the right as he could. "Any minute now."

He pulled the ratchet handle a few more times. Even though I was braced for it, the gunshot-like sound of the bolt coming out and the door slamming into the truck bed made me jump again. Shawn was able to hold on to the ratchet this time. He climbed down off the truck and walked over.

"Okay, let's get a lead rope on the horses," Erica said. "I don't think they'll be too bad, but let's get a handle on them before we move the truck, just to be on the safe side."

Monica's daughter ran around to the tack room and came back with two leads. She handed one to Erica, and they leaned in through the windows and attached them. Once that was done, Shawn climbed up in the cab of the tow truck and pulled it forward out of the way. The horses remained calm, and Erica carefully pulled the right-side door open. It shrieked in protest as the bent hinge reached an angle that it didn't like, but it opened enough to get the horses safely out. The left door swung out without a problem.

"Okay, let's go Aztec, back it up." Monica stepped forward and took charge, and the bay gelding began backing off the trailer. "That's a good boy, keep it coming."

Aztec's rear feet began the familiar short-step dance of a horse that knows he's close to the edge of the trailer but can't tell how close. At last, he made it off, and Monica grabbed his lead rope and handed it to her daughter.

"Take him into the wash rack so Dr. Lacher can check him out. I'll grab Frenchie." Monica climbed in the trailer and opened the divider to the front slot. Frenchie stood there nice and calm, as if he'd been snoozing in his stall instead of in a trailer wreck with an explosive rescue. She stepped up and pulled the rope off his shoulders and clucked her tongue. "Come on, old man. Let's back it up."

Frenchie slowly backed off the trailer. I couldn't see any sign of injury on him, and there didn't appear to be any bloody spots or smudges on the trailer walls. Shawn and I followed them into the barn, where Erica was already looking over Aztec. She stepped out and watched Frenchie walk down the aisle, then returned to her exam. Monica put Frenchie on the crossties across from them, and Erica came over to check him out a few minutes later.

"I think they're both fine, honestly," she said as she finished up. "Neither one of them walked in lame from the trailer, and I didn't palpate any sore spots. I'm sure they're both a little banged up, and they'll probably be sore for a few days, just like you or I would be, but they seem like they did okay. We'll put them on some pain meds so they feel better. That's a happy ending for a trailer wreck, though, about the best that it can go."

Monica's shoulders sagged in relief, and she turned and wrapped her daughter in a hug. "Ugh, this has been the worst day, but that's the news I needed to hear." She stepped back after a moment and wiped her eyes. "What a nightmare!"

"Hopefully you at least had a good ride," I said, trying to find a bright spot for them to focus on.

"We never even got there!" Monica said. "We were still on the way to meet Sue. Sue! Oh gosh, I need to let her know everyone's okay." She yanked her phone out of her waistband and began typing. "The last she knew, we were waiting for the cops to get there. She's probably worried to death."

Once the horses were safe in their stalls, we headed back out front. "I've got an old guy down in a pasture," Erica said. "I need to get headed to that, but if anything they do today makes you worried that something else is going on, let me know."

Monica pulled Erica into a side hug as they walked out into the sunshine. "Dr. Lacher, I don't know what I'd do without you."

Erica smiled and pointed at Shawn. "He did all the rescuing today, I was just a spectator."

"And he put on a good show," I added. "Very dramatic!"

Shawn laughed. "That was way too much drama for me, thanks. I'm just glad the horses are okay."

Monica released Erica and gave Shawn a hug. "No, you were definitely a hero today. Thank you for coming, and for being so considerate of the horses. That means a lot to me."

We all parted ways, and Erica and I headed back across Paynes Prairie towards Ed's farm. I was relieved that Snooter didn't need to be seen. This was already more action in one day than I was ready for.

Before we had gone a mile, Erica's phone rang again. I glanced at her with a raised eyebrow, ready to turn around and head back if it was Monica. Erica shook her head.

"Hello, Dr. Lacher."

"Dr. Lacher, it's Edward Stanton again."

"Hi Edward. I'm just leaving the emergency in Micanopy and headed your way."

"Well, I might have jumped the gun on that," Edward said. "Old Milton stood up about fifteen minutes ago, and he's been wandering around grazing like business as usual. Do you think he was just tired this morning?"

"This is how it goes for a lot of old guys," Erica said. "It gets harder for them to get up, and one day they just can't do it, and that's it. My guess is that even if today isn't that day for Old Milton, he's letting us know that it's coming."

Edward let out a deep sigh. "I sure have a hard time telling you to come put him to sleep when he's standing there eating grass like he always does. But I don't want him to lay out there all night and me not know about it, either."

"It's a tough spot," Erica agreed. "One of my old guys went out that way. I went out to feed breakfast, and he was down in the pasture. You could tell from the hole he dug that he was there all night, and his head was all skinned up. I felt horrible about it, but sometimes there's just nothing you can do. I would tell you that if he looks okay, and he's moving around, then it's reasonable to leave him alone for now. Just keep in mind that this is going to happen again, so you need to keep a closer eye on him."

Edward was silent for a minute, and my heart went out to him. Making the decision to end a life is the hardest thing you can do, for a lot of us. Most of the time, there's no clear answer that it's the right thing to do. It's a decision that's made and then second-guessed until we either find acceptance or we drive ourselves crazy.

"Well, since this is the first time it's happened, let's wait and see how he does," Edward said at last. "I know Carol would want him to be happy, so the next time he can't get up, we'll do it then."

"I think that's very reasonable," Erica said. "Just make sure you put eyes on him two or three times a day."

I turned west on Archer Road and started back towards the house. Our flurry of emergencies had gone from one to three, then back to one. It felt like a busy morning, regardless. We were still sitting at the red light before the interstate when the phone rang again.

"Hello, Dr. Lacher."

"Hi, it's Cindy King. One of my clients is on the way home from the Horse Park, and her horse is down in the trailer. They're on the Alachua exit ramp of I-75. I'm in Orlando, so I can't do anything. Can you help her out?"

I immediately put my blinker on and started creeping into the on-ramp lane for the interstate as I watched for an opening. A moving truck went by, and I slipped behind it and headed north as Erica gathered some details on what was happening.

"Okay, we're actually only about fifteen minutes away," Erica said, opening her laptop. "Which horse is it?"

"Birdie Bird is the one that's down. That's the horse

Kristy's leasing from a lady in Alabama. Kristy said Ivan was kicking her while she's down. He's one of mine, of course. She's trying to get Ivan off the trailer before he hurts Birdie any worse. I've got contact info for Birdie's owner, and I'll send you Kristy's number too, so you can talk to her directly."

Unloading a horse on the exit ramp seemed dubious to me, but I wasn't there to see what was going on. I tried not to be judgmental, but the risk of a horse getting away and running around on I-75 made me queasy. I probably would have taken the extra minute to drive to a parking lot, but again, I wasn't the one dealing with the crisis and trying to make decisions in the heat of the moment.

Erica's next call was to Kristy at the scene. She sounded out of breath, but more composed than I expected.

"Hello?"

"Kristy, this is Dr. Lacher. I just got off the phone with Cindy, and we're headed your way. You're on the northbound exit ramp in Alachua, correct?"

"Oh, hey. We're actually pulling across the street into the McDonald's right now. The cops are blocking traffic so my daughter can walk Ivan across the road."

My stomach did another slow roll. The road at the bottom of the ramp was Highway 441, which is a divided four-lane. There were so many things that could go wrong, and only one thing that could go right. It was a recipe for disaster.

"Okay," Erica said. "Is Birdie still down in the trailer?"

"No, she got up as soon as we got Ivan backed out. I don't know how bad she's hurt. She's got bloody scrapes all over her legs, but she seemed okay standing on all four feet. I was just afraid to put Ivan back on the trailer in case he attacked her again. Right now, I'm trying to get everyone over in the corner of the parking lot so we can figure out what to do."

"Do you have someone who can come pick Ivan up and get him home in a separate trailer?"

Kristy sighed. "I called the one person I can think of and left a message, but everyone else I know from Lake City was at the horse show with us, and they've all got a full trailer."

I did some quick math in my head, calculating travel time if we had to go home and get the truck and trailer to go pick up this horse. We were twenty minutes from home, and the house was twenty minutes from the McDonald's. Allowing a few minutes to hook up the trailer, it would be forty-five minutes before we could get there. That seemed like forever in a situation like this.

"I have a client right around the corner from where you are," Erica said. "I can see if she'll come get Ivan, or she can bring Birdie to the clinic and you can take Ivan home, or whatever makes the most sense."

"Oh my God," Kristy said. "If she could bring Birdie to you, that would be amazing. I need to call her owner and tell her what's going on, too. She's going to lose her mind."

Erica chuckled. "Okay, we'll head straight to the clinic, I'll call her, you call the owner, and I'll call you back and we'll go from there."

The changing plan happened at a perfect time, and I got off at the next exit instead of proceeding to Alachua. Whether we had to go get the truck and trailer or just go to the clinic, this was the best way to get there. Erica was already on the phone again by the time we got to the red light at the bottom.

"Hi Nancy, this is Dr. Lacher. This is a strange request, I know, but are you home and able to haul a horse to the clinic for me? I've got an emergency happening at the McDonald's in Alachua, and I need transport."

Nancy was a seasoned horse person, and took the call in stride. "Sure, I can do that. I just got off of Topper, so let me get him unsaddled and in a stall. I can be there in about fifteen minutes."

"You're the best," Erica said. "I'll text you her number in case you have trouble finding each other, but just look for the horse standing in the McDonald's parking lot next to a trailer."

"There can't be too many of those there," Nancy said with a laugh. "I'll let you know when we're headed to the clinic."

I felt a bit of sympathy for Erica's phone as she called Kristy back. It was getting a serious workout this morning, even more than usual.

"I've got a trailer coming in fifteen minutes," Erica said. "Nancy Jennings is on her way to pick up Birdie."

"Okay, great." Kristy sounded tired. "I just talked to Martha. She wants you to call her once you've looked at Birdie. I'll pay for everything, but she's worried about her horse, of course."

"It's tough to be an absentee owner in an emergency," Erica said. "I get it. Cindy gave me Martha's number, so I'll call her as soon as I can."

"Thank you for all your help with this," Kristy said. "It's been a disaster of a morning."

"I'm glad to help," Erica said.

It was after eleven-thirty when we got to the clinic.

We had about fifteen minutes before Birdie would arrive, so I made a bowl of ramen noodles. Years of experience had taught me to always keep emergency food at the clinic, and to eat it when there was an opportunity. The way this day was going, it might be hours before I had another chance, and I'm not a great help to anyone when I'm starving. Quite the opposite, really. Erica opted for a piece of leftover pizza from the fridge, and we sat down in the aisle and shared a quiet lunch.

Nancy pulled in with Birdie just as we finished eating. Erica went out to get Birdie off the trailer, and I wheeled the ultrasound out to the aisle just in case she needed it. We had no idea what kind of shape the horse was in, and our approach is to prepare for the worst and hope for the best. The x-ray machine was inside too, but I decided not to drag it out until Erica asked for it.

I waved at Nancy as she drove by the barn door. Erica walked Birdie into the aisle and stopped at the crossties. The horse was moving okay, at least as far as I could tell, which is to say that she wasn't three-legged lame. Her chestnut coat was covered in bits of shavings and poop from where she'd been on the trailer floor, and her white stockings were crisscrossed with bloody scrapes.

"If you want to just stand here and hold her, I'll check her out," Erica said. "I don't know how she is about crossties. Be ready to move with her if I find a painful spot."

I took the lead rope as Erica began her exam. She started at Birdie's head, running her hands all over her face and jaw, then down her neck and back. Birdie stood still, head hanging. Erica ran her hands down each leg, then lifted each foot off the floor and flexed the joints.

"This is pretty much a pre-purchase exam, huh?" I said.

"Pretty much. I have to figure out if she's hurt anywhere other than these scrapes."

Once she was done palpating everything, she brought the ultrasound machine over. I watched the screen as she slowly moved the probe over the lower legs, but the only thing I could really tell was there didn't seem to be any distended small intestine in the hocks and fetlocks. Reading the ultrasound wasn't one of my strong points.

"I think it's all superficial," Erica said at last, rolling the cart back out of the way. "There's some swelling on the left rear hock area, though. Let's take some radiographs of that just to make sure there's nothing broken in there."

"Okay. She's pretty quiet, can I put the crossties on her?"

Erica nodded. "Yes, I think she'll be fine with it."

It took a few minutes to get the x-ray machine set up. This was our newest machine, and everything was cordless on it, even the plate. That was very exciting for me, as I lived in fear of a horse stepping on the cable of our other machine, which would probably cost a small fortune to replace. Since I didn't do this stuff all day, every day, I had to constantly think about all the things; where is the cable in relation to the horse's feet, am I holding the plate straight, is my lead vest in the right position while I'm squatting down, can I move if the horse moves, and so on. It's a lot to keep track of, so having one less major component was a big deal.

"Bring the top of the plate towards me," Erica said, lining up the generator with the fetlock. I move the plate slightly. She hit the button and the computer beeped. "Okay, move it up to the hock. I want to get the whole bony column."

My job was to hold the plate square with the generator.

Top and bottom, left and right, and the diagonal angle, all while leaning over and holding it from one side. Erica was on the other side of the horse, so I could barely even see the generator. By the third image, we were in a groove.

"Take the right side out an inch. The other right. A little more. Hold it right there." The computer beeped again. "Okay, let's see what we got."

We stepped over to the computer screen. Erica enlarged the images and carefully looked them over. Unlike the ultrasound, I could clearly tell what I was looking at, at least in terms of what was a bone and what wasn't. Hairline fractures could be extremely difficult to spot though, so I didn't trust myself to interpret what I was seeing.

"Well, she's got some arthritis," Erica said, pointing to a sharp point on one side of the hock joint. "That should be round. But I don't see anything bad. I think she's just a little banged up. I'm going to give her some pain meds, and I think she'll be fine in a few days."

"Well, that's great news," I said. "I'll put all this stuff away while you start calling everyone."

By the time Erica had talked to the owner, the trainer, and the person leasing the horse, and explained her findings and the treatment plan to each of them, I had all the equipment put up and the horse in a stall with water and hay. We closed down the clinic and headed home.

"I don't know about you, but I'm ready for a nap." I turned on to our driveway, willing the phone not to ring for at least an hour, preferably two. "This has been a morning."

"For sure," Erica agreed. "I guess this is what we get for not having a single emergency yesterday."

"That's fair," I said. "I'm not sure if I'd rather have all

the emergencies at once, or have them spread out over the weekend. There's some pros and cons to both."

It had been a wild morning. So many horses had been in potentially life and death situations in the last few hours, and they had all walked away mostly unscathed. It didn't always work out so good for everyone, but it was really satisfying when it did. I even managed to get a nap, and all was good in the world.

10

Pet Walks the Line

There are few things in this world that I love more than our donkeys. Erica has had Teacher's Pet, or Pet, for short, for close to twenty years. Hannah Banana, the retired circus donkey, came to us in 2016, which you'll recall from the first book in this series (unless you haven't read it yet, in which case there is a thorough history of the donkeys waiting for you there!).

I've pondered my attachment to them at length, trying to decide what it is that draws me to them in such a powerful way. They don't listen to me at all. They do whatever they want to do, which is often the opposite of what I want them to do. They're fiercely independent. And yet, for all that, they love to hang out with me when I'm working on their fence or trimming trees. They will stand quietly and let me brush them for hours. And even though they get pushed around by the horses when they have to share a pasture, they still rebel against the power structure in their own way and maintain their dignity. I don't know if I love them in spite of these things, or because of these things. Or maybe it's both.

One morning, I went out to the back pasture to feed the donkeys and sheep as I always do. They don't really need much in the way of feed, so we just give them a handful to keep them tame and approachable, especially the sheep, and to give Hannah her medication. Gerald and Tweak, our two sheep, are both obese, so they don't actually get more than a couple of pellets each, but they are adamant about getting them. Hannah has equine asthma and Cushings, so she gets a squirt of steroid and a pill in her feed to keep her functional. The four of them meet me at the gate every morning without fail. So, when Pet was missing from the group, I knew right away that something was wrong.

It was wintertime, so it was still dark. I went ahead and fed Hannah and gave her morning meds, then ran back to the barn to get a flashlight. Erica was putting the last two horses in their stalls for the day when I got there.

"Perfect timing," I said. "Pet didn't come up for breakfast. Want to help me find her and see what's going on?"

"Uh oh. That's not good." She hung all but one of the halters on the rack by the feed room door. "Let me grab my headlamp."

The donkeys had both back pastures at their disposal at the moment, which was about five acres altogether. With giant live oak trees dotting the landscape, it was a lot of space to search in the dark. We split up, with Erica taking the left pasture, and me taking the right.

After eight years, I knew the donkeys and their favorite hangout spots. For example, when Hannah Banana doesn't feel good, she always goes to the back fence line and stands under a particular cedar tree. Every time she's had an asthma flare up, or an abscess in her foot, she always goes to that tree. I think it makes her feel safe when she's vulnerable.

Pet had never been unhealthy since I'd known her, but she still had her favorite shade tree where she hid from the scorching sun or the pounding rain. It was in a small copse of fir and pine trees, a tiny natural fort with a couple of branch stubs poking out at just the right height for ear scratching which were polished smooth from years of use. I decided to start there.

Tweak and Gerald followed me across the pasture, and Hannah trailed behind them. I shined the light around as we trudged through the yellow grass, the powerful beam cutting through the darkness all the way to the woods on the other side of the fence. Off to my left, I could see Erica's headlight bobbing around in the adjoining pasture.

I reached the donkey fort and ducked under the low-hanging branches, shining the light in front of me as I entered. The space was empty. I turned around to leave, but the sheep were in the way.

"Go on," I said, nudging Tweak with my knee. "Where's Pet hiding?" It took some shuffling, but the sheep managed to get turned around and out of the way just as Hannah arrived. I scratched her ears as I pointed the light at the back fence, slowly moving from the right corner to the left. Pet was nowhere to be seen.

I walked down to the front fence where the water bucket sat, swinging the light back and forth as I went. No sign of Pet. My last guess was a cedar tree that sat right on the fence between the two pastures. It was also an ear-scratching favorite, and a place she might have decided to hole up if she was sick or hurt.

Erica was on the far side of the other pasture, her headlamp moving back and forth like a lighthouse as she made her way from the back to the front. We had covered a lot of the space by this point, and I was really starting to worry that we hadn't found her yet. If anyone was going to break out and escape, it would be Hannah Banana, and that only left a few bad possibilities on the table, the kind I wasn't even willing to consider for more than a few seconds.

The tree was still thirty feet away, but Pet was clearly not there. I stopped and turned in a slow circle, trying to light up every inch of the pasture. I was almost back to my starting point when a dark shadow in the grass caught my eye. I moved closer. It was a low spot in the pasture, an old roll hole that often held rain for a few days. The tall grass around the edge obscured my vision until I was right on top of it.

Pet was laid out flat in the roll hole, perfectly hidden in the dark. Her sides were heaving, so I knew she wasn't dead. I waved my light back and forth as I shouted to get Erica's attention.

"I found her! Over here!"

Erica was a couple hundred yards away, and her light flashed and bobbed as she jogged towards the gate. I turned back to Pet. My biggest fear was that she'd been attacked by coyotes. It wasn't something that happened much in our area, but we heard them howling at night sometimes, and our sheep were probably a tempting meal choice. The donkeys were naturally aggressive towards dogs and coyotes, which made them great protectors for the sheep, so it was possible that Pet had gotten hurt while trying to save Gerald and Tweak.

Pet rolled her eye back to look at me as I ran the light across her. There wasn't any blood or obvious signs of injury that I could spot. The grass was all mashed down around her, so she'd been here for a while and had done some thrashing. I put my hand on her flank, but she didn't even raise her head. Erica arrived a moment later.

"Pet, what have you done to yourself?" she asked. She ran her hands across Pet's legs, carefully checking for broken bones. "Do you have an abscess?"

"She hasn't tried to get up at all," I said. "It looks like she's been here for a while, though. Should we roll her over?"

"I think so," Erica said. "I'm not sure what's going on. Let's flip her and see if we can get her up."

When rolling horses, you have to use ropes, because they're just too strong and heavy to do it without them. No matter how tough you are, a horse can pull his foot out of your hand and kick the snot out of you. Pet was only about a third of a horse in size and strength, and while it was still a risk, it was a manageable one.

"Grab both legs so she doesn't kick you," Erica said, mirroring me on the front end. "We're going to lift the lower leg. We're just holding the upper leg so she doesn't kick us with it."

"Got it," I said. I stuck the flashlight in my pocket and reached down and grabbed both back legs at the same time.

Pet struggled feebly in my hands, but not enough to get away from me.

"Ready?"

"Yep."

"Go."

Lifting the lower leg and not the upper was harder than I expected. Pet kicked her legs as we pulled, and it took all my coordination to restrain with my left hand and restrain *and* lift with my right. It didn't help that we were going up the side of the roll pit, even if it was only a small incline. As always happens when turning a horse over, we reach that magic point at the top when gravity took over for us, and Pet flopped over on her other side.

"Let's drag her away from the edge so she's on flat ground," Erica said.

I grabbed her feet again, and we tugged her over a few feet. Pet snorted twice and rolled up in the sternal position as soon as we let go.

"I don't think she liked that very much," I said.

"I'm just glad to see her voicing an opinion," Erica said. She gave Pet a quick exam on this side, running her hands over every inch in search of an injury. There was a raw spot above her eye from rubbing the ground as she struggled, but that was it. "We'll give her a minute to get some circulation going, and then we'll try to get her to stand up so we can see what's going on."

Erica turned her headlamp off, and we stepped back a few feet to give Pet some space. Hannah Banana was grazing nearby, and the sheep came over to get some attention from me. Tweak stood beside me and curled her head around my leg, and I scratched her neck. This was her favorite thing in the world, other than stealing a bite of food from the bucket. Now that the lights were off, I realized that the sky was beginning to brighten.

After a few minutes, Tweak wandered off to inspect some weeds near the fence. I glanced at Erica, and together, we stepped back up beside Pet. Erica slipped the halter on her and tugged gently on the lead rope. Pet didn't move, so I nudged her in the ribs with my knee as Erica tugged again. This time, Pet lurched to her feet, wobbling from side to side as she attempted to regain her equilibrium. I put a hand on her hip to steady her.

"Well, that's not good," Erica said, switching her light back on. Pet was holding her front left leg up in the air. "Do you want to hold her for me?"

I stepped around her and grabbed the lead rope, not that Pet was trying to leave. Erica palpated the hanging leg, trying to find something tender or abnormal. When she got down near the knee, Pet snorted and swung her head at Erica. I shortened the lead rope before she could make contact.

"Now, now," I said. "None of that. She's just trying to figure out what's wrong so she can make it right."

Erica worked her way down to the foot, and stood up. "We need to get her up to the barn so I can ultrasound her. I'm pretty sure she's blown a tendon."

"Oh, no," I said. "I was hoping for an abscess."

"Me, too." She switched her light off again. "Let's see if she'll take a step forward."

I pulled on the lead rope. Pet resisted for a minute, but she finally hopped forward on her right leg. I backed up another step, turning towards the gate, and she hopped forward again. After three more hops, I stopped and let her rest.

"It's going to take us a while to get to the barn," I said. "Why don't you go ahead and get the coffee going and set up the ultrasound machine, and we'll meet you at the barn."

"Okay, good idea. I'll message the clinic and let them know I'm going to be late to work this morning. Do you think you can get her through the gate without bringing the whole crew?"

I shrugged. "Probably. But even if everyone comes, that's not necessarily bad. Maybe if Pet sees Hannah grazing in the yard, that will encourage her to keep going."

"Fair point."

Erica took off, and I coaxed Pet another five hops. It was slow going, but I didn't want to hurt her good leg by wearing it out while she was completely unwilling to put weight on her bad leg. This was already a troubling situation. Horses can only be on three legs for so long before they get into serious trouble. Donkeys have a little more time, as they're considerably lighter, but it was still a potentially life-threatening situation, and I wouldn't be able to live with myself if I accidently killed my donkey by rushing her to the barn.

The sheep were waiting for me at the gate, and Hannah trotted up as soon as I opened it. I didn't bother trying to keep them in. The gate swung wide, and everyone rushed out except for Pet, who hobbled slowly behind. Once past the gate, she stopped to graze, as everyone knows that's where the grass is always greener. Hannah Banana and the sheep were several yards ahead of us, and I stopped to admire the pink streaks in the sky as the sun crept towards the horizon. A moment later, Erica came back out and gave Pet a shot.

"That'll make her feel better," she said. "But don't push her."

"Got it."

It took us about twenty minutes to get to the barn and onto the wash rack. Erica was finishing a bowl of cereal when we arrived, and pointed to another one sitting on the table next to a steaming mug of coffee as I clipped Pet to one of the crossties.

"I figured you were starving, since I was."

"That's why you're the one," I said with a smile.

Erica soaked Pet's leg with alcohol and began the ultrasound exam while I slurped down breakfast. Pet stood quietly, head hanging. It didn't take long for Erica to determine the problem, and she stood up with a deep sigh.

"What is it?" I asked.

"Superficial digital flexor tendon. It's pretty common for older horses to tear it."

"What does that mean?" I asked, my appetite suddenly gone. "Can she recover from it?" Pet was twenty-four, which technically made her a little old lady, but I was completely unprepared to lose her.

"Yeah, she'll probably be okay, but it's going to be a long couple of months for her." Erica shut down the ultrasound machine and disconnected the probe. "She's going to have to live in a stall, and she might founder."

Thoughts raced through my mind, too fast to even acknowledge. Would Pet be able to handle living in a stall when she'd spent her whole life in a pasture? Would Hannah have to live in the stall with her to keep her company? Would the sheep be okay out in the pasture without the donkeys? Was there some way to rig a sling so Pet could stand without foundering on her right foot? Was it fair to ask her to go through all this at her age? The coffee that had been so welcome a few minutes before was turning to acid in my stomach.

"How should we do this?" I asked, trying to avoid bombarding Erica with all the things I wanted to ask at once.

"There's very little we can do other than support her and keep her on pain meds. This is one of those things the body has to fix by itself. The injury isn't that big of a deal, really, the tendon will grow back. What kills them is that they either founder from standing on three legs too long, or they lay down too much and get giant bed sores everywhere that end up getting infected, and you can't get ahead of it. But a lot of them don't want to lay down, because it's hard for them to get up, and they feel too vulnerable."

"Well, she was laying down in the pasture, so maybe that's good," I said. "Should we roll her over a lot, then? Like you would for a person?"

"Yeah, for sure," Erica said. "But we also need to keep her stall as clean as possible so she's not laying in urine and poop, especially when she has open sores."

I thought about how much of my day this was going to consume, and then immediately felt guilty for weighing Pet's wellbeing against my time. My therapist's voice flashed through my conscience, asking me how to reframe this as a positive thing. It wasn't hard, once I changed my perspective. I worked from home most of the time, so this would be a good way to get away from my desk and move every few hours, which is something that I struggled to do consistently. Pet was going to help me as much as I was helping her.

"Alright kiddo," I said, scratching Pet between the ears.

"Let's go check out your new digs for the next few weeks."

"I bedded out the empty stall and filled the water buckets," Erica said. "It's all ready to go."

"Perfect." I unclipped Pet from the crossties and backed slowly down the aisle. She hopped into the stall and immediately went to work on the flake of hay in the corner. Erica had bedded the stall much deeper than normal, and I hoped it would be enough to keep the bedsores at bay. As I turned around to leave, I found Tweak poking her head in the door.

"Pet, you have a visitor," I said. "But you'll have to make it quick, visiting hours are over in five minutes."

Pet ignored Tweak and continued working on the hay. The timothy was a treat for her, as she normally lived on grass, or grass and coastal hay in the winter. A pair of tall gray ears came into view in the window, and I hustled over to the door. If Hannah came in and started helping herself to the hay, I'd never get her back out in the pasture.

True to their nature, Tweak and Gerald had already managed to both pee and poop in the barn aisle. We'd had enough sheep running around the farm for me to know this was a favorite activity of theirs, even if I didn't understand it. I grabbed a feed bucket and put a handful of grain in it, and lured Hannah and the sheep back out to the pasture. My coffee was cold when I finally got back to it, but I finished it anyway.

I spent the first week developing a new routine. Pet established right away that she was not going to spend much time on her feet. Erica and I would stand her up at morning feeding, and she was usually back down by my nine a.m. walkthrough. I would roll her over at eleven and one, stand her up at three, then roll her again at five and seven. We would stand her up again at nine, right before bedtime.

The bedsores started on day five. The first one was on her left hip. I discovered it when I rolled her over, which I had gotten good at doing by myself out of necessity. Knowing this was coming, Erica had left a tube of diaper rash ointment on the windowsill. I smeared some on the quarter-sized red spot, and paid extra attention to finding the wet areas as I cleaned her stall.

By day ten, she was covered in bedsores on both sides. None of them were infected yet, so that was good, but it seemed inevitable. The ones on her hips were bigger than my hand, and we were going through ointment at a record pace. She still wouldn't stand up on her own, and I was finding it harder and harder to convince myself that she was going to pull through this. She looked like a trainwreck. Her bedsores were covered in diaper rash ointment, and the ointment was covered in shavings, which stuck to it like Velcro. She had lost a lot of weight, but that wasn't all bad, as she had been considerably overweight at the outset. Still, it was difficult to watch.

I found myself spending more and more time with her. I would bring my laptop down and sit beside her and sort through emails while she munched on hay. Her body was a disaster, but her eyes were still bright, and she hadn't lost her enthusiasm for eating. It was during this time that I discovered how soothing it could be to sit in a barn full of horses while they're eating hay. The birds outside created a nice backdrop to the sound of chewing, along with an occasional snort. It was a very peaceful thing, something that most horse people probably knew forever, but that I was just discovering.

Erica and I had a stall-side meeting at the two-week mark. We'd spent the better part of an hour cleaning all of the bedsores and reapplying fresh ointment. Every joint and point had a raw spot by then, and each day they grew deeper and wider. I was starting to understand what Erica meant about not being able to stay ahead of them.

"This is really looking bad," I said, leaning against the window ledge. "Is it actually bad, or does it just look that way?"

Erica sighed. "Right now, it looks worse than it is. Nothing's infected yet, and that's the thing we're watching out for. But that could change in a day, and then she'd be in big trouble. But she also isn't standing up on her own, and that's not good."

"How long do we let this continue?" I asked. "Do we put a time frame on her for standing up, or do we go by the bedsores? I don't know what the protocol is for this sort of thing."

"It's not easy," Erica said. "It depends on a lot of factors. If she keeps losing weight, she's going to get to the point where she doesn't have enough muscle mass to stand up. But since she's not standing and moving around, she's going to keep losing muscle. It's a race between that and the sores getting infected, really. I'd say she needs to be standing on her own by the end of the week, or else we call it."

I felt like throwing up. It's much harder to be objective about euthanizing your own animals, and I had a strong emotional connection with Pet. I didn't want her to suffer pointlessly, but I found myself struggling to separate my own selfish desires from the truth of her condition. When I was honest with myself for a second, I knew she wasn't doing great, but the thought of ending her life unnecessarily if she could still make a comeback was abhorrent. I was glad Erica had the knowledge to make a judgment call on that, because I didn't think I could do it.

Two nights later, we were doing the nine p.m. stand up and stall cleaning. I emptied the wheelbarrow and brought a fresh flake of hay in as Erica finished reapplying ointment to the spots that needed it. We stopped outside the door and watched Pet munching on hay for a moment. She turned and limped over to the water bucket, and Erica let out a squeal of delight.

"Did you see that?" she asked. Her face was glowing, but I had no idea what she was so excited about.

"What? What did I miss?"

"She just walked over to the water bucket," Erica said, as if it were the most obvious thing in the world. "On both legs! She's putting weight on her bad leg."

It finally dawned on me. "Oh! Oh! That's great! That means she's healing the tendon, right?"

"Right!"

My spirits soared. The dread of her impending demise had been a constant weight in my gut for days, and in that moment, I realized just how fully I had come to believe that she wasn't going to make it. This was an unexpected beacon of hope.

The next morning, Pet was laying down, as usual. Erica and I rolled her over, and for the first time in nearly three weeks, she stood up all by herself.

"This is so exciting!" I wanted to wrap my arms around her, but there wasn't a big enough spot to hug her without rubbing on a bedsore, so I settled for scratching her ears. "I'm so proud of you! Can we take her out to the little paddock so she can eat some grass?"

Erica shook her head. "Easy, killer. She just started putting weight on it last night. Let's give her a few days before we ask her to walk a hundred yards."

"Of course," I said, mildly chagrined. "We don't want to undo the progress she's made."

The following morning, Pet was standing up when we got downstairs. I felt like she'd heard us talking about going out to the paddock and was trying to show that she was ready for it. She still spent most of the day laying down, but I could tell that she was standing up on her own based on where she was in the stall, and which side she was on.

That Saturday morning, we decided to go for a test walk. Pet limped slowly out of the stall, the first time in twenty-one days, and hobbled down the ramp. The winter rye grass in the paddocks was bright green, and she set her sights on it immediately. The limp on her left leg was pronounced, but it was holding up so far.

"Should I slow her down?" I asked. "I don't want her to blow the tendon right back out. Her head is bobbing like crazy."

Erica shook her head. "Nah. The pain pill hasn't had time to kick in yet, so she's feeling most of it. That will keep her in check."

We made it to the small paddock near the barn, and I took the lead rope off her halter and stepped back. Pet immediately went to work on the grass. Seeing her out in the sunshine made me realize just how much weight she had lost. She looked terrible, but watching her stand and graze made me feel like the worst was behind her. Her bedsores were finally starting to heal, and she'd managed to avoid getting an infection that might have changed the course of her future. The line between life and death was very fine, and she had been perilously close to crossing it.

"Okay, let's let her hang out here for the day," Erica said. "We'll bring her back in this afternoon."

I carried the water bucket over to her so she wouldn't have to cross the field to drink. Throughout the day, I went out to check on her. Several times I found her lying down, but always in a different place. From the large patches of grazed down grass, I could tell she was excited about being out there.

That afternoon, I slowly walked her back to the barn. She wasn't in good enough shape to defend herself if she needed to, so we felt it was best to keep her in the stall at night. This became the new routine, out in the little paddock in the daytime, in the stall at night. On the fourth day, I brought Hannah Banana and the sheep up to spend the day with her in the little paddock.

I guess I expected a big reunion to take place, with lots of braying and prancing around. Hannah walked in the gate, and as soon as I took her halter off, she found a place to graze, and never even acknowledged Pet. To be fair, Pet didn't pay any attention to her, either. Gerald and Tweak ran around scoping out the weed selection. I stood at the gate and watched them for a while. There were never any theatrics, but gradually Pet and Hannah Banana drew closer together as they munched on grass, and after a half hour, they were side by side. It was subtle, but I felt like it was the older donkey version of a joyous airport reunion between family members.

We waited another week to turn Pet out back in her pasture with the others. She was still limping, but a bit less each day, and her bedsores were getting noticeably smaller. As I led her out of the stall for the last time, she stopped in the doorway and pooped. I felt like it was a fitting goodbye to her home for the past month.

It took another month for her limp to go away completely, and nearly six months for all of her bedsores to heal over and grow new hair. By summer, she had put a lot of weight back on, and was even starting to get chubby again. If you didn't know what she'd been through over the winter, you'd never realize what a close call she'd had just by looking at her.

Life returned to normal, as it always does. It's hard to maintain a sense of appreciation for the lives and good health of everyone around us, but sometimes I have a moment of clarity that pulls me out of my complacency, and I'm grateful. The older I get, and the older our animals get, the more I realize what a gift the good days are.

11

Quincy and the Kid

Over the years, our veterinary practice has grown and changed a lot, and the demands on Erica's time have mirrored that. Recording new episodes of our podcast, *Straight from the Horse Doctor's Mouth*, answering questions from Patrons of the podcast in our Facebook group, filming videos for our YouTube channel, writing blogs for the website, being a guest on other podcasts and YouTube channels, co-authoring an academic book, and presenting workshops at equine veterinary conventions all added up to more hours than were available in a weekend. It was also making it really hard for her to ride her horse more than once a week, and she wasn't happy about that. The solution? We decided that instead of seeing horse appointments four days a week, we would drop it to three.

We had three other veterinarians in the practice to help carry the load, so on paper, it seemed like we could come in for the staff meeting on Friday mornings, and then go work on whatever the project of the day was. It was logical to me, anyway. The office staff stopped scheduling appointments for Erica on Fridays, and we started making the transition.

The flaw in this plan, which I began to understand in retrospect, was letting Erica go to the clinic for the staff meeting. Once she was there, a million things would demand her attention, and she would spend most of the day there anyway. It started out with paperwork and returning phone calls to clients about various things. Then it was breeding season, and she had to pitch in and ultrasound mares, order semen, and all that stuff. And, because she was available, she would end up catching whatever emergencies happened so the schedule wouldn't get messed up for the other doctors.

So it came to pass that we were at the clinic one Friday morning, long after the staff meeting had ended. Erica was on the phone with a client discussing lab results, and I was plotting out the next month's seminar topic with Melinda, our office manager. The phone rang, and a few minutes later, Lisa, the receptionist, popped her head into the office.

"I've got a new client with an abdominal laceration hauling in from Salem. Do you think Dr. Lacher can see it?"

"Where is Salem?" I asked. "I've never heard of that."

Lisa closed the office door and pointed to the map on the wall behind it. "It's way over here by the Gulf Coast, north of Steinhatchee, on the way to Perry. It's tiny."

I looked at the time and sighed. Salem would be an hour

drive or more, especially with an injured horse in the trailer, which meant they wouldn't arrive until noon. Depending on how bad the laceration was, that would take an hour or so to manage. Assuming we went home right after that, say one-thirty, we would have about two and a half hours to set up the cameras and lights and shoot a video before Barbara, our barn person, arrived to feed the horses and clean the stalls. That was a tight window, but we could get it done. Probably.

"Yeah, we'll manage it," I said, glancing at the packed schedule on my computer screen. The video was important to me, but not so much that I was willing to lump the emergency onto one of the other doctors and keep them out working until eight on a Friday night.

A full schedule was both a blessing and a curse. On the upside, there weren't any wasted hours in the day with staff sitting around doing nothing. As the guy in charge of keeping us in business, slow days were physically painful for me. For every hour that we weren't earning income, the remaining hours in the day needed to make even more for us to break even on costs. It only took a few slow days in a month for us to go in the hole, which was why my beard turned gray when I was forty.

The downside to a full schedule was that there was no room for emergencies without throwing everything into chaos. And there's some sort of rule in the universe that decrees that the fuller the schedule, the more emergencies you will have. An empty schedule will never have an emergency. That's just the way it works.

Desi was the in-house tech that day, so I helped her get things ready as noon approached. We knew that the horse had a big flap of skin hanging from the belly, and that it was dirty, so we put lots of chlorhexidine gauze and sterile saline on the cart, along with suture supplies and drugs. We rolled it out into the aisle just as a truck and trailer pulled in the gate.

I opened the big doors at the end of the aisle and walked out to the trailer to help them unload. The back doors of the pickup opened first, and a teenage girl climbed out, followed by a smaller teenage girl. A young boy popped out the other side, and then another one behind him. They all sported bright red hair and freckles, and I began to wonder if the flow of kids was going to stop.

The front doors opened at the same time. A thin man with bright red hair and a shaggy red beard got out the passenger side, holding a baby carrier, and a woman with strawberry blonde hair and tired eyes got out from behind the wheel. The seven of them trooped back to the trailer, half on each side, and formed a line behind it. I felt like I was in a movie about the Irish potato famine. A voice in my head began doing a scene, complete with the thick Irish accent. "*Aye, it's Nellie, she's all we've got left. Can you save her, sir?*" I squashed a laugh before it could come out.

"Alright, who do we have here?" I asked.

The oldest girl stepped forward. "This is Quincy. We just got him a couple weeks ago. He's my horse."

"And mine," her little sister piped up. "We're sharing him."

Not to be left out of the excitement, the smallest boy jumped up and down. "I want a horse!"

"Hush, Sophie. Let Ava handle it. Everyone be quiet so Ava can talk to the vet." Her mother smiled at me apologetically. "I'm Mary. We're teaching Ava how to manage things."

"That's good! And I'm not the vet, just a technician." I grinned at Ava, then glanced down at my clipboard. "Quincy's a two-year-old gelding quarter horse, right?"

She nodded. "He's not great at being handled yet, but we work with him on the halter every day."

"Okay, that's important, thank you. Do you know if his vaccines and everything are up to date?"

Ava glanced back at her mom uncertainly for a moment, then turned back to me. "I don't know. The guy we bought him from got him at an auction last month. He was supposed to have his Coggins, but the officers at the ag station said the papers we have aren't a real Coggins. It says that the auction has his Coggins, but we have to go ask them to get it, or something. It's weird."

"Yeah, there's a lot of sketchy things that happen at auctions," I said. "It's best to assume he hasn't had anything recently, then. I'm guessing you'll want to get a Coggins while you're here so you can get him home once we patch him up."

She looked to her mom again, who took over for her. "Yes, we'll want to get everything he needs," she said.

"Got it." I patted the trailer door. "Let's get him unloaded so we can see what's going on. Do you want to handle him, Ava? Desi's really good with young horses if you'd rather let her do it. It's totally up to you." I pointed to Desi, who was waiting off to the side.

"She can do it," Ava said with a shy smile, stepping back.

I opened the trailer door, and Desi popped out a moment later with a palomino horse. A dirty triangle flap of skin the size of a saucer hung down from the center of his belly. She led him over to the water hose, and the rest of us followed.

"Quincy, what did you do to yourself?" I asked.

Sophie was quick with an answer. "He tried to jump out of the round pen so he could be with the other horses."

"Hhmm, looks like he didn't quite make it."

"Yes, he did," Sophie corrected me. "He tore his belly open, but he got over the fence. Ava and me had to go catch him."

"I'm glad you were there to take care of him." I grabbed the hose and turned on the water. "Everyone stay back, he's probably not going to like this very much."

I started with his foot, and slowly moved the stream of water up his leg. Quincy danced around, but Desi kept a tight grip on the lead rope, moving with him and applying side pressure to get him back in the middle. When the water hit his belly, he reared up, pawing the air. I immediately pulled the hose away, and Desi got him back on the ground.

"Well, time for drugs," I said. I kept my tone easy, but on the inside, I was shaking a bit. If Quincy had been just a bit more aggressive, he could have really hurt Desi, and I didn't take that lightly. "I'll be right back."

Inside the clinic, Erica was at the counter typing on her phone. "We're going to need you to sedate the horse," I said. "He reared up at the water hose, and I didn't even get to the laceration. And I only had a two-second glimpse, but I don't think he's actually a gelding."

"Oh, sounds like fun," Erica said, handing me her phone. "Let's go grab some drugs. If Dr. Maddox texts me back, let me know what she says. We're trying to make a plan for a laminitis horse."

When we got out to the horse, Desi was teaching Ava and Sophie how to calm Quincy down when he was too excited. "Just remember that he's mirroring your behavior. If you're calm, he's calm. If you're freaking out, he's freaking out. You have to be in control of yourself in order to be in control of him."

"I knew that," Sophie said. "I'm going to clicker train him to do tricks."

"Clicker training is a great tool," Erica said. She eased up beside Quincy and put a hand on his neck. "We use it to teach needle-shy horses how to stand still for a shot, and to get them to load on a trailer. I'm Dr. Lacher, by the way. Is this Quincy?"

"Yep. He's my horse." Sophie shot a venomous glare at Ava. "And my sister's. We're sharing him."

"It's very nice of you to share a horse," Erica said. She slipped the needle into Quincy's neck. He gave no reaction other than a slight head twitch, and the shot was over in a second. "It looks like he's already a good boy for shots."

"He wasn't very good for the hose," Ava said. "He wasn't like that when I washed him at home, though."

"His belly is probably really sore, and he's trying to protect it," Erica said. "In this situation, it's not that he's being bad, he just doesn't want it to hurt worse. I just gave him a shot that will make him sleepy so we can wash it without anyone getting hurt."

The little boy piped up from the other end of the line. "I want a horse!"

"Hush, Phillip. You don't know as much about horses as I do." Sophie stuck her tongue out at him.

"Sophie!" Her mother's voice cut off any further discussion.

Quincy's head was starting to droop, so I grabbed the hose again for another try. He still danced around some, but nothing like the first time, and I was able to get a steady stream of water on his wound. I kept the pressure low and worked back and forth between the belly wound and the hanging flap.

"Why's it taking so long to get clean?" Sophie asked.

"We usually try to wash out wounds for ten minutes," Erica said. "There's dirt and sweat and all that stuff on it, but there's also all kinds of bacteria that was on the outside that can get inside through the cut, so we want to wash away as much of that as possible. Have you ever heard the saying, *dilution is the solution to pollution*?"

Sophie giggled. "Dilution pollution?"

Erica smiled. "Dilution is the solution to pollution. That means that if there's a bunch of bad stuff in a small spot, like the injury on his belly, we can make most of the bad stuff go away if we wash it with enough water. That way his immune system has a better chance of fighting off what's left before it becomes infected."

"I knew that," Sophie said.

Ava snorted. "You did not, you're such a liar!"

"Girls, we're not doing this here," Mary said. Her voice was even, but her tone left no room for argument. "Dr. Lacher's trying to teach you something. Pay attention, or you can go sit in the truck."

When Erica was satisfied that I had hosed the wound long enough, we walked Quincy into the barn aisle. She put her headlamp on and bent over to take a closer look. The injury was nearly on the centerline of his abdomen, and there didn't seem to be any way to safely treat it with him standing up. She probed the wound, checking for any deep punctures.

"Okay, I think we're dealing with a superficial injury," she said, turning her light off as she stood up. "The good news is, it's not a serious wound, even though it looks terrible. The bad news is that we're going to have to lay him down to get it sutured."

"Why is that bad?" Ava asked.

"It's not *bad* bad," Erica said. "But any time we have to anesthetize a horse, there's always a risk that something could happen, just like with people going into surgery. It's a very small risk, and 99% of the time, it's fine. The other reason I say it's bad is because it's going to cost a bit more to get him patched up."

Ava nodded, accepting the explanation. Erica was probably right for being vague with the kids about the risks of dropping a horse. Technically, there was a possibility that the horse could die, and statistically it happened to a little over 1% of horses who were anesthetized for surgery. We wouldn't be doing gas anesthesia, as he only needed to be out for a few minutes, and we had never experienced a death in a surgery, but it was always possible. The bigger risk for Quincy would be waking up. As a prey animal, his instincts would be screaming at him to stand up in case he needed to run away or defend himself, and while he was still groggy, he could fall badly and break a leg. That was always Erica's biggest fear, and we worked extra hard to keep them on the ground as long as possible to let their head clear and their balance improve.

"We're going to move Quincy into this stall right here,"

Erica said, pointing behind the family. You all are welcome to stand at the window and watch, but nobody can be inside the stall except for me and my technicians, okay?"

"Okay." The chorus of responses ranged from excited to disappointed.

"I can't see in the window," Phillip said. "I want to see!"

"I'll get you a stool to stand on," I promised. "It looks like we'll probably need one for a couple of you."

Desi led Quincy in the stall, and Erica went inside to gather the necessary drugs and supplies. I went out to the shed to see what I could find for the kids to stand on. The step stool we kept by the stocks would work for the taller one, but I needed something higher for Phillip. I started to grab a folding chair, but then my eye fell upon the cooler that we used for drinks at Open House. Perfect!

By the time I got everyone arranged at the window of the stall, Erica was back and ready to go. She gave Quincy another shot, and when his head was drooping down to his knees, she gave him a third one. Desi hurried out of the stall, leaving Erica to manage his head as he crumbled slowly to the floor.

Guiding a thousand-pound horse into the position you want him as he's losing consciousness is not always a simple task, but Erica made it look easy. She pushed Quincy's head to the right just after his front legs buckled, and he rolled onto his right side. Once she was sure that he was out, she waved us in.

"Let's pull him away from the wall just a bit," Erica said, still holding Quincy's head up off the floor. "Justin, grab his back legs, Desi, you grab the front. If he starts to kick, just let go and get back."

The three of us grunted and strained, and Quincy slowly slid over. It took a few tries, but we got him scooted over about a foot. I was glad that he dropped more or less straight down so we didn't have to go far. Sometimes they stagger around the stall, and we have to work a lot harder to get them in position.

Desi and I grabbed a few bags of bedding out of the corner and lined them up beside him while Erica put a towel over his eyes and tucked it into his halter to keep them protected. This was one of the scariest parts for me, because we would be at our most vulnerable while we rolled him over on his back. Desi grabbed his front leg, the one closest to the floor, and I grabbed the corresponding back foot. Erica moved around behind the bags of bedding and prepared to shove them into place.

"Everybody ready?" Erica asked. "Okay, roll him."

Desi and I lifted, grunting and straining together. Quincy slowly flopped over onto his back, the wall preventing him from going on over. As soon as he was up, Erica slid the bags of bedding up against his ribs, bracing them up under him as tight as they would go. I was officially stuck in place, holding his back feet up until it was over. The bedding would mostly keep him in place, but it wasn't 100%, and we couldn't risk him sliding back over in the middle of the procedure.

Desi and Erica went into high gear. Now that Quincy was out, the clock was ticking, and every second counted. They slid a palpation sleeve, which is the clear plastic glove that goes up to your shoulder, over each foot to keep dirt from falling down on his abdomen. Desi rolled the cart of supplies over beside him, then took her spot at his head. She was in charge of monitoring his level of sedation and breathing, and giving him a bump dose if he started to wake up too soon, as well as keeping his front feet from flopping over or getting in Erica's way while she worked.

Erica put on a pair of rubber gloves, and squatted down to assess the situation. "You said they told you he was a gelding, right, Ava?" She glanced over her shoulder at the crowd filling the window.

"Yes, ma'am."

Erica pointed to a large bulge between his back legs. "That right there is a testicle. And it looks like there's only one, which means he's probably a cryptorchid." She palpated the area, probing around in search of a second testicle. "Definitely only one. So that's not good news."

"Why's he got one?" Sophie asked.

"That means the other one is up inside his abdomen, and it will require a surgery to get it out," Erica said. "And since I can't feel it anywhere, it's probably deep inside, so he'll have to go to a referral hospital to get that done. But this also explains why he wanted to jump the fence to get to the other horses. He's a stallion."

Mary let out a deep sigh, and I knew exactly how she was feeling in that moment. Whether intentional or not, the horse they'd bought for their kids had been misrepresented. Now they were stuck with it, and all the bills that were going to come as a result. On top of that was the problem of his temperament as a stallion, and whether or not he would be appropriate for small kids. "Do I even want to know how much that will cost?"

Erica shrugged. "It all depends on how long it takes them to get it out. They're usually not too bad, maybe $1,200, maybe less."

Mary's husband spoke up for the first time. "Well, that might have to wait a while. This right here is probably going to cost more than horse did."

"You don't want to wait on that surgery," Erica said. "The longer he stays a stallion, the more events like this you're going to have to deal with. The alternative is putting a lot of money into your farm to make it stallion-appropriate, and in terms of cost, you're way better off just getting the surgery done as soon as possible."

"That makes sense," Mary said, shooting her husband a glance. "None of our fences are in great shape. If he managed to jump out of the round pen, none of the rest of them are going to do much to keep him in."

"The round pen is taller than me and Ava," Sophie said.

"And me!" Phillip added. Even standing on the cooler, he could barely see over the window ledge. "I want a horse!"

Erica used the clippers to remove the hair around the edges of the wound and the skin flap, then set to work scrubbing and cleaning everything. Now that I could see it, I realized that it wasn't nearly as bad as it could have been. The skin had ripped, but that was it. The muscle underneath wasn't affected, and that was a big deal. Sometimes horses get hung up on a fence post and basically eviscerate themselves, and that's a lot harder to fix. By comparison, this was small potatoes.

Once everything was clean, it was time to sew it up. She put a clamp on the point of the triangle and stretched it forward, covering the wound completely. "Justin, can you hold this in place while I suture it?"

"Sure." I leaned forward and grabbed the clamp with my right hand, twisting slightly so I could keep a hold on his foot with my left hand while not leaning directly over the laceration. It took about a minute for my back to start complaining, but by then she was halfway up one side. Erica can sew like a machine when she has to, and she wasn't messing around. She finished the left side and was working on the right when Quincy took a deep breath and let it out with a sigh.

Desi moved the towel and peeled his eyelid back. "He's still pretty out, but he's starting to wake up. Do you want me to give him a bump?"

"No, I think we can get done. I just need a couple more minutes."

I hoped she was right. If Desi had to give him more drugs, we'd be waiting around for another twenty minutes for him to wake up. My back was starting to get serious about protesting, but Erica knocked out the last few sutures and took the clamp from me a moment later. I leaned back carefully, wondering when I had gotten so old and fragile. The change in position was all I really needed, as it turned out, and by the time she was done, I was back in decent condition.

I helped Erica clear everything out of the stall. When the cart was outside, we pulled the palpation sleeves off Quincy's feet and moved the bedding bags back to the corner. I tried not to rush it, but I was anxious to get him back over on his side and get out of kicking range as fast as possible since he was waking up.

Erica grabbed his front foot, then glanced at me and Desi. "You all ready?"

I nodded, and pulled his back foot over toward the center of the stall. I could feel him pulling against me, but not very strong. He flopped over at last, and I released his foot and backed away. Desi stayed by his head, keeping the towel over his eyes and a hand on his neck as Erica and I headed out of the stall. The goal was to keep Quincy on the ground as long as possible to give him the best shot at standing up safely.

Erica pulled her gloves off and turned to the family. "Okay! That went really well. I'm going to give him a couple of vaccines before he gets up, and then he'll be all done. What did you guys think?"

"That was fun!" Sophie said. "I'm going to be a vet."

"Me, too," Phillip said, jumping off the cooler. "I want a horse so I can roll him over! I'll do it every day."

Erica laughed. "Well, you get to practice taking care of Quincy. I'm not going to bandage him, because it's really hard to do there. Instead, I put silver sulfadiazine, or SSD, on it, and you're going to run a water hose on it twice a day while it heals. I'm going to send you home with some SSD, but I don't know if he's going to let you put it on him. I definitely don't want anyone getting kicked, so this is probably an Ava or a mom job."

"Thank you," Mary said. "And thanks for your advice on the cryptorchid surgery. Can you help us get that set up?"

"You bet," Erica said. "Let me just vaccinate him quick, and then we'll give them a call."

Once they were inside the office, the rest of us turned back to the stall to watch Quincy wake up. He was taking a lot of deep breaths and blowing them out, and Desi was working harder to keep his head on the floor. I knew it wouldn't be long now. After a few minutes of tail swishing and blowing, he let out a shrill whinny.

"He's awake," Sophie announced. "That's how he sounds when he's ready to eat."

Desi made sure the lead rope was stretched out beside her, and slowly removed the towel from his eyes. Quincy blinked a few times, and sat up, looking around like he was lost. Desi spoke softly to him, holding the rope with one hand and patting his neck with the other. They sat there for a few minutes.

"Why's he sitting down?" Phillip asked.

"He's still pretty sleepy," I said. "It's just like when you wake up in the morning. Sometimes it takes a few minutes to get your head screwed on straight before you get up."

"I never want to sleep," Phillip said. "I want a horse. I'm going to ride him all the time, and I won't have to share him with Sophie 'cause he'll be mine."

I didn't know what to say to that, but Quincy rescued me. He stuck his legs out in front of him, and Desi stepped back out of the way. With a sudden burst of effort, he lunged to his feet and stood there swaying back and forth. Desi worked to steady him, keeping a short lead on him so he didn't try to walk right away. They stood there in silence as he recovered his equilibrium.

By the time Erica and Mary came back out, Quincy was eating treats from Desi's hand, and the kids were running around the barn. Erica stepped in the stall and gave him the vaccines, and Desi carefully walked him out to the aisleway. Mary's husband was already back in the truck with the baby, and I wondered if I could survive a day in his shoes. Some people thrived in a big family like that, but it was way too much energy for me. Of course, he would probably find my life way too quiet and still, so there was that.

Desi loaded Quincy back on the trailer, and we all said our goodbyes. I knew Quincy would never be able to appreciate how fortunate he was, but I did. Lots of horses in his situation would find themselves back at another auction, sold to someone else who would find themselves in this same situation, or worse. The fact that he had a family who was willing to do what needed to be done was a blessing, and I was grateful on his behalf. It was a good reminder that there can still be a happy ending for horses in bad situations. They just need to meet the right kid.

12

Absentee Technician

I didn't meet Erica until I was 38, which was in 2014. Before that, I was gathering all sorts of life skills so that I'd be properly suited to be her husband. Part of that experience involved being in a relationship with a woman named Kari from 1998 until 2009. She was a wonderful person in many ways, and taught me more than I could possibly explain. She was nine years older than me, and while it was my first real relationship, it was not hers.

Kari brought two things to the relationship that are relevant to this story. One was Lupus, and the other was Nathan, her son. Nathan was ten when I met him. He was mentally handicapped, and while he could walk and talk and generally handle himself, he couldn't read or write, and he had a serious stutter that made him difficult to understand. Kari had developed toxemia while she was pregnant with him, and he ended up being very premature. The prognosis for Nathan wasn't good at all, but he beat the odds and did all the things he was never supposed to do.

Nathan and I had a rocky start. He was very protective of his mom, and he was still dealing with the fact that his dad was in and out of his life at very irregular intervals. Adding me into the mix really stretched his emotional bandwidth. We slowly became a family unit though, and as we spent more time together and I learned how to communicate with him, our bond formed. I taught him a few things, and he taught me a lot of things, and somewhere along the line, we became joined at the hip.

Nathan and I spent a lot of time playing guitars, playing video games, fishing, and riding my motorcycle. Over the years, my connection with him grew much stronger than what I had with his mom. A lot of that was due to my own issues that I hadn't dealt with back then. And some of it was on Kari, and her challenges. We were both imperfect people, and we didn't have the tools to overcome those things, so we drank a lot.

Kari and I split up in 2009, about a year and a half after I got sober, but Nathan and I continued to hang out. He saw a lot of Georgia from the back of my motorcycle, attended band practices, and generally had a good time. In 2013, Kari moved to Arizona with her new boyfriend. Even though Nathan was 24 by then, he still lived at home, so he was along for the ride.

Things didn't go well for Kari. In 2014, her boyfriend

beat her up worse than usual and put her in the hospital. They separated, and Kari and Nathan eventually ended up in a small apartment, trying to put their lives back together. I talked to Nathan on the phone once in a while, but not very often. It was a really hard time for them, but I was in a new relationship with Erica by then, and there was an entire continent between us.

Kari found a ranch for mentally handicapped adults and got Nathan in as a daytime participant. It was a great place for him to be, as they had a ton of social programs and physical activities to keep Nathan engaged, which was way better than sitting around watching TV all day. It also gave Nathan a safety net, which proved invaluable when Kari had a stroke, her third. It put her in a nursing home, and Nathan became a full-time resident at the ranch. Kari never recovered from that, and she died in 2022 just before her 56th birthday.

What does all that have to do with horses? Nothing, at least on the surface. But when Kari died, Nathan needed a guardian, and I felt like there was no one better suited than me. So, after talking to Nathan's grandmother, I hired a lawyer, filed all the paperwork, and started traveling to Arizona to get everything handled.

My first trip out there was just before Christmas. I hadn't seen Nathan in person in nine years, and I felt guilty about that. But once I arrived at his door, he gave me a huge hug, and we were immediately plugged in like we'd never been apart. His hair was thinner and receding, but otherwise he was the same old Nathan.

I was sitting at his kitchen table on Saturday morning, chatting with his caretaker while he finished breakfast. My phone dinged in my pocket, and the chime told me it was the clinic Chat. Erica was on call that weekend, and it was the first time in our eight years together that I wasn't there to be her on-call technician. The phone dinged again, and I pulled it out, reassuring myself that it was okay that I was here and not there.

Dr. Lacher: Anybody available to come help me at the clinic? I have a choke coming in that's not resolving, could use a hand.

Desi: I can be there in ten minutes.

"Who was that?" Nathan asked.

"That was our group chat for the vet clinic," I said. "Erica has a choking horse coming in, and she was asking if any of the techs can come help her out with it."

"A choking horse?"

I nodded. "It's different when horses choke, because they can still breathe. Food just gets stuck in the food pipe."

"It gets stuck? How?"

"It's usually because the food is dry, and they need it to be wetter. Sometimes they don't have enough saliva to swallow right."

Stephanie, Nathan's caretaker, chimed in. "It's amazing how well you understand him. I think I'm the best translator he has here, and I don't catch half of what he says."

"Years of practice," I said with a grin. "Me and Nathan go back, what, twenty-four years, kiddo?"

"And, and, and he was my stepdad," Nathan said, struggling past the stutter. "And now he is again."

"That's right." I ruffled his hair. "You want to watch the horse emergency? I can bring up the cameras on my phone."

"Yeah, I'll watch it." He shoved a spoonful of scrambled eggs in his mouth. "I'll watch anything, like, like, like football or a movie."

"I see you're still talking with your mouth full," I said with a chuckle. "Take your time, we gotta wait for the horse to get to the clinic."

"I have to remind you about that all the time, don't I, Nathan?" Stephanie asked, smiling to soften the chastisement.

Nathan pointed to his full mouth and grunted.

"Now he's back on track," I said. "Let me grab my laptop out of the car and I'll see if I can get the video on that so everyone can see."

I got my laptop set up on the table and hooked my phone to it just in time to see the truck and horse trailer pull into the clinic. John and Danny, Nathan's two roommates, came over to watch, and we all gathered around the screen.

It was a strange feeling to watch Erica working an emergency while I was two thousand miles away. I kept fighting off the recurring stab of guilt in my gut. Knowing that Desi was there, and that she was a far more capable technician than me, did nothing to make me feel better about it. I distracted myself by explaining what was going on.

"That's Erica, standing by the door," I said, pointing to the screen. "She's the doctor. Desi is walking over to the trailer to help unload the horse. They're going to bring her inside and put her in the stocks, which is this metal frame box thing here. Once she's in, she can't move around too much, and they'll stick a tube up her nose and down her throat and pump water in there to clear out the food she's choking on."

"Tube up her nose?" Nathan said. "I, I, I wouldn't like that in my nose. No thanks!"

"Me either," I said.

Desi led the horse inside the door, and I switched

camera views. There was no audio, but I could still imagine the ringing sound of pipes banging as she walked into the stocks and Desi shut the rear gate behind her. Erica slipped her stethoscope in her ears and began listening to various parts of the horse.

"What is she doing?" John asked.

Before I could respond, Danny jumped in. "She's listening to his heart. My doctor does that to me all the time. And the microphone is cold, but I'm tough and I just sit there."

I laughed. "That's right! She's listening to the horse. She'll check the breathing, heartbeat, gut sounds, everything, so she knows for sure what's going on. I can tell that Danny's a pro at this."

Danny beamed, his eyes shining through his thick glasses. "I go to the doctor all the time. My mom says I should work there because I know all the stuff, but I'm going to be a fireman."

"That sounds like more fun," I said.

On the screen, Erica was wrapping up her exam. The horse turned her head to the right, and the long trail of drool hanging from her muzzle caught the light. That was a pretty solid indication that it really was a choke, at least to me, but Erica would always do an exam to make sure there wasn't more to the story.

She turned to the table under the camera and lifted a bottle of clear liquid, inserting a needle into the cap and drawing up a few cc's of whatever it was. It was pure chance, as she didn't know we were watching, but the syringe was right in the middle of the screen and caught the light just right. A chorus of reactions filled the room around me as the group of guys who probably received many more shots than the average person took in the spectacle.

"That thing is huge!" Danny shouted. "I've never seen a needle that big!"

"Wow," John agreed. "I'm glad I'm not that horse!"

"And," Nathan said, holding up a finger, "And, and, and, it's a big horse."

"A big horse gets a big needle," I said, nodding in agreement. Nathan could be very perceptive about things, and he was pragmatic to his core. It didn't surprise me that he was the one who was unimpressed by the size of the syringe. "That's probably sedation, which will make the horse sleepy so they can work on it. Horses don't like it when you stick a tube up their nose, so you have to make them sleepy first."

Desi was filling a bucket with water, and the owner was standing in front of the stocks, scratching the horse's ears as the drugs began to kick in. Erica pulled out the nasal-gastric tube and coated it with lube, and Desi met her at the front of the stocks. The owner stepped back a few feet.

"Erica's going to put the tube up her nose now," I said. "The horse will probably swing her head around some. But once she gets it in there and they start pumping water, it's going to get messy. A lot of the food that she's choking on is going to come back out her nose with all that water, and she's going to start sneezing big globs of goop everywhere."

"Messy," Nathan said with a grin, clapping his hands. "It's going to get messy!"

Erica put a hand on the horse's nose to steady her head, and started to insert the tube. A moment later, the horse reared up on her hind legs and lunged forward, getting her front legs over the chest bar before dropping back down. Erica and Desi scrambled to get out of the way of the thrashing hooves. I couldn't tell from the camera angle if anyone got kicked or not, but from the way they were moving, it looked like they were okay.

Erica ran around the horse to the table and grabbed another needle and more sedation. The owner was all the way across the aisle, her hand across her mouth. In that moment I was glad there was no audio, as she was probably screaming along with her horse. My heart was hammering in my chest, and I was doing my best not to panic. Nothing like this had ever happened before, and the one time it did, I was absolutely helpless to do anything. Not that I could have done much if I was there, mind you, but that wasn't a conscious thought at that point.

Erica was unflappable, as always. She got beside the horse's shoulder, out of range of the still-flailing front feet, grabbed the lead rope, and managed to stick the vein with one hand on the first try. Desi came and took the lead rope, and Erica disappeared around the other side of the horse. I thought about switching cameras to try and see what she was doing. Now that the initial shock was wearing off, I was running through all the possibilities I could come up with on how to handle the situation. It was a very short list with no clear answers.

A moment later, Erica reappeared at the back of the horse, and I realized she was opening the stocks. The way our stocks are designed, the side bar can swing out, which will let the chest bar fall. As soon as she pulled the back pin, I knew what her plan was, and it was far simpler and more effective than anything I had come up with.

"The chest bar is going to drop," I said, remembering that I had an audience who had no idea what was happening.

"The horse might fall down here, but let's hope not. This is a very unusual situation, but Erica is going to get the horse unstuck."

A second later, the horse dropped to the ground. Her legs buckled and she dropped to her knees, but Desi was ready for it. She kicked the chest bar out of the way and kept her grip on the lead rope as the horse jumped back to her feet. They walked forward out of the stocks and stopped in the middle of the aisle.

Now that she was out of the stocks, the horse was calm. Her head drooped, and the double-dose of sedation seemed to finally be working. Erica cautiously ran a hand down her side, but she didn't react.

"What's she doing now?" Nathan asked.

"I think she's checking to see if the horse got hurt during all the kerfuffle," I said. "She's putting her hands around the horse's belly where she was stuck on the bar, and feeling her legs. Veterinarians do a lot of feeling on horses, which they call palpation, or palpating the animal. They palpate them, or feel them, to see if something feels hot, or swollen, or even broken."

"My doctor palleted my leg when I broke it," Danny said. "It hurt pretty bad, but I'm tough."

"Palpated," Stephanie said. "You were very tough, especially when you got a shot to stop the pain."

"I didn't like that shot," Danny said. "But my leg hurt worse. And I did better than this horse did! I didn't even move very much."

"That's pretty awesome," I said with a grin. "This horse wasn't even hurt; she just went crazy!"

"Yeah! I'm tougher than a horse!"

Stephanie pointed to the screen. "It looks like she's going to try the tube again."

Sure enough, Erica was putting lube on the tube again. Desi stood on the opposite side and held the lead rope. I was the most nervous I've ever been when Erica put her hand on the horse's nose and began inserting the tube. The stocks at least offered some containment and protection, but now they were just standing in the aisle. If the horse reared again, there was nothing to keep her from injuring people.

The second round of drugs seemed to do the trick. The horse tossed her head a few times, but she kept all four feet on the floor. Once the tube was in as far as it would go, Erica took the lead rope, and Desi brought the bucket of water over and attached the hose to the pump.

"Now we're finally to the part where things are going to get messy," I said. "She's pumping water down the horse's throat to where the food is clogging it up. Most of the water and food is going to come back out her nose, and she's going to sneeze and spray it everywhere."

"Messy!" Nathan said, clapping his hands in anticipation. "Time to get messy!"

"Gross," John said, shuddering. "Is it going to get on them?"

I nodded. "Yep. It's almost impossible to keep from getting sprayed once she starts sneezing."

A moment later, lumpy water started to trickle out of the horse's nose and pool up on the floor. I kept waiting for Erica or Desi to warn the horse's owner, who was standing a few feet in front of them, but their focus was on the horse, and rightfully so.

The first sneeze was a whopper. The horse's head

moved forward and down as her neck stretched out, and her owner was instantly covered in slimy goo. She scrambled backwards, but it was far too late for that. Erica's left arm was coated up to the elbow as well, and I could see spots all over her pant leg. Desi probably had some as well, despite being off to the side, but I couldn't see her very well due to the camera angle. Beside me, a chorus of reactions were taking place.

"Whoa!" Danny shouted. "She got slimed!"

"Yeah!" Nathan clapped his hands enthusiastically. "Messy!"

Even Stephanie couldn't help but chuckle at the spectacle. "She's going to have to hit her clothes with the water hose before they can go in the laundry."

Water and feed continued to pour onto the floor, and a few smaller sneezes followed the first one. Suddenly, the flow slowed to a trickle, and Erica began pushing the hose down the horse's throat again.

"There it goes," I said. "That means the blockage is gone, and she's pushing the tube all the way to the horse's stomach, just to be sure there isn't another one."

"And," Nathan said, "And, and, and, how do you know it's in the stomach? You can't see inside."

"Watch," I said. "Erica's going to put the end of the tube in her mouth and blow on it. If she's in the stomach, it will be like blowing into a straw in a glass of water. She'll feel it blowing bubbles. If it's not in the stomach yet, it will just be like blowing through a straw in the air with no back pressure."

"Blowing bubbles in her stomach?" Nathan asked incredulously. "And, and, I wouldn't let her blow bubbles in my stomach. It might make me, you know, toot the gas." He pointed to his butt, and everyone in the room cracked up laughing.

"Well, as long as you chew your food before you swallow, you probably won't have to worry about that." I ruffled his hair with a grin.

"I will," he said solemnly.

Desi pumped the remaining water into the horse, and carefully pulled the hose out. The aisle was a wreck, and I didn't envy her the cleanup that was coming. Having been the tech in that situation many times myself, I knew there was probably a spackling of feed and snot all over the walls, and maybe even on the ceiling. Chokes were always a mess.

"So, that's it?" Stephanie asked. "It seems so anticlimactic."

"Yep, the dramatic part happens early on. Very dramatic, in this case. But the clearing part is usually pretty low-key. The only other thing that happens sometimes is a bloody nose if they fight the tube a lot."

"A bloody nose," Nathan repeated. "Messy!"

"Definitely messy," I agreed.

On the screen, Desi was walking the horse outside, while Erica and the horse owner headed to the sink in the corner to wash up. I shut the computer off and closed the lid, wishing I could call Erica and talk about the insanity of what had gone down. That would have to wait, as she still had to do billing and help Desi wash everything down.

It's hard to be a human sometimes. We have all these irrational urges and feelings, and we don't always know what to do with them. I knew, on an intellectual level, that nothing would have been any different had I been there in person to help Erica with the emergency. I couldn't have managed the horse any better than Desi, and probably not as well by a large margin. But knowing that didn't stop me from feeling like I had let Erica down in some way, or lessen my desire to race home and be there for her on the next one.

I tried to steer my thoughts in a positive direction. All the drama had certainly been a break in the routine of everyone's lives here at Nathan's house. Nathan and his roommates would be telling stories about it for a long time to come. And I got to see that the world could go on without me, which was an important lesson for me to remember. Taking care of Nathan and spending time with him did not mean I was leaving Erica helpless, even if it felt that way. She had been doing this long before I met her, and her superhuman abilities and her support team would get her through anything that happened while I was gone.

Nathan and I went out for ice cream. I sat across the table from him and watched him eat with the same mannerisms he'd always had (napkin square with the edge of the table, pushing his glasses up after every bite, attention focused solely on the food). Being there made me nostalgic in a way. It was hard to fathom how much my life had changed in the thirteen years since his mom and I had split up. In some ways, I felt like I was in two overlapping worlds at the same time, but the Justin of 2008 was a completely different person from the Justin of 2022.

Now that I was back in his life, I was going to have to find a way to merge those worlds together. And that was a task I could get excited about! By the time I finished my root beer float, I was already planning Nathan's first visit to our farm. We had a lot to catch up on, and I couldn't wait to introduce him to Erica and all the animals. A whole new chapter in our lives was just beginning!

13

The Adventures of Vincent van Goat

Sometimes animals get themselves in situations they can't manage. And sometimes, they get their owners in situations *they* can't manage, either. That's usually a very bad day for everyone involved. But every once in a while, we find a happy ending to a bad situation.

For example, there's a very spoiled horse who lives in Ocala, Florida named Miracle. When he was just a few weeks old, he injured his eye pretty seriously. His owner didn't have the money to send him to a referral hospital to get it fixed. Rather than euthanize him over it, which was the owner's plan, we found someone who was able to raise the funds to pay for his care, and he became her horse. He had a rough few months of living in a hospital in the beginning, but since then he's been under the careful management of a little girl who loves him very much, and they're both thriving.

For Vinnie van Goat, it was a similar story, except that he was an adorable little black and white goat instead of a horse. When he was about six weeks old, he climbed up on a pallet. His back left foot slipped down between the slats just as he fell off the side of it, and he broke the snot out of his leg.

He was standing in a wire dog crate in the aisleway at our clinic the first time I saw him, his leg hanging awkwardly and very definitely broken. Despite the injury, his eyes were bright, and he was eating a long piece of hay, which stuck out the side of his mouth in a way that made him look like he was auditioning for the role of Tom Sawyer. My heart immediately leaped out of my chest, and when he looked at me and let out a little baby goat bleat, I was finished.

"Hey, little fella," I said softly, dropping to sit beside him on the floor. "What did you do to yourself?"

His face was solid black, with a band of white freckles across the bridge of his nose and around the edge of his huge ears. He bleated again, then went back to work on the hay. Somehow, he didn't seem to be aware of his leg. I was glad that he wasn't suffering, as I don't think I could have handled that. I hung out with him for a few minutes until Dr. Hanks arrived with Lexi, her tech, the goat's owner, and an armload of bandaging supplies.

"Ah, I see you've met Winchester," she said with a smile. It's common knowledge around the vet clinic that if a baby goat is within a mile, it will draw me in like a moth to a flame. Apparently, that's my siren song.

"We were just getting acquainted," I said.

"Well, since you're here, you can help us splint his leg."

My face lit up. "You bet! It looks like he did a number on it."

"Oh, wait until you see the x-ray," she said. "He did several numbers on it."

I grimaced at the thought. "Poor little guy. You must be miserable, even if you don't look like it."

"He's already had some drugs," Dr. Hanks said. "It's probably still sore, but nothing like it was."

"Well, that's good news," I said, scratching his chin through the wires. "He's so cute I can't hardly stand it."

Lexi organized the supplies, and Dr. Hanks and I unclipped the roof of the cage so we could extract the goat without banging his leg around. I pulled the roller chair over so I could sit and hold the goat while they wrapped his leg. When everything was ready, I lifted him out and we got to work.

"Okay, let's turn him to face you," Dr. Hanks said. "We need his bad leg pointed out at an angle like this so we can get to everything."

"Got it." I spun the goat around carefully. He was still working on the piece of hay and didn't seem to be very interested in what we were doing.

"So, you're not going to put a cast on it?" the owner asked.

Dr. Hanks shook her head. "No, at this age, they grow so fast we'd have to cut it off and replace it every other day. With the splint, you can rewrap it instead, which will allow the leg to grow as it heals."

"Oh, I see."

She got the two pieces of broken bone straight with each other and carefully began to wrap the leg. The splint was a variety of layers and went from his hip to his hoof. The outside layer was bright yellow vet wrap. It made a fantastic contrast to his black coat, and he was ridiculously cute when they got finished, but I doubted it would stay clean for long. Having been through this process with Gerald, our sheep, I knew how grungy it could get in a day, even living in a stall.

"Let's let him walk around for a minute and make sure everything is okay," Dr. Hanks said as she stood up and stretched her back. Winchester, as his owner called him, wandered off a few steps, his splinted leg hanging out to the side like a bright yellow rolling pin. "I think it's okay. We're going to take another x-ray with the splint on, just to check the alignment of the bones. As long as everything looks good, he'll be ready to go home."

Lexi rolled the x-ray cart over and grabbed the plate, while Dr. Hanks hefted the generator. I held the goat up in the air, and they took a couple of images at different angles. Winchester was content to let us do what we needed, and quietly chewed on the hay stem. I decided he wasn't actually eating it, since it wasn't getting any shorter.

"We got it mostly aligned," Dr. Hanks said, turning the screen so the owner could see it. "But that doesn't mean it's going to stay that way. Since it doesn't have screws or anything holding it together, we're relying on the splint to keep the two ends of the bone close enough for them to grow back and reconnect. I know that surgery isn't an option for him, so when you change his splint wrap every other day, you have to make sure the bones stay aligned so they don't miss each other. I'd like to bring him back in a few weeks and take another x-ray, just to confirm it's doing okay."

"I wish I had the money to do the surgery," the owner said. "I barely make any money on them as it is, and the surgery would cost more than all my goat sales for the year."

"I get it," Dr. Hanks said. "This is a tough position for any animal, and especially for production operations. One bad thing happening throws a big wrench in everything."

I realized that Winchester was bred to be a meat goat. As a boy, the only monetary value he had was what he could be sold for on the meat market. Female goats could be kept to breed more babies, as well as produce milk for various products, which gave them a little more wiggle room in situations like this, but it was hard to justify spending a thousand dollars or more on an animal that could only be sold for a hundred bucks. Winchester was in a bad spot.

We sent him home with a box of bandage material. It was hard to watch him leave, even if he did have a decent chance of healing properly. Just knowing that more could be done for him if money wasn't part of the equation hurt my soul. But there was a limit to what we could do without putting ourselves out of business, which would prevent us from helping any animals at all. This was a thought process I had to go through on a regular basis, even though I reached the same conclusion every time. Sometimes things have to go this way.

Two weeks later, Winchester was back. I couldn't believe how much he had grown in such a short time. He was sporting dirty blue vet wrap on his leg, and once we got him out of the crate, I saw that he wasn't using the leg at all. I tried to remember how fast Gerald, our sheep, had started using his leg once it had been splinted. It seemed like it was right away, but time has a way of distorting such things.

Once the x-rays were taken, we gathered around the screen to assess his progress. It only took a glance to see that things weren't good.

"The good news is that he's laying down a lot of new bone," Dr. Hanks said. "The bad news is that they aren't connecting. They're growing past each other."

The owner's face fell. "Is there anything we can do?"

"At this point, the only thing we have is amputation. There's no way to realign the bones without cutting the new growth off, and that's not really a viable option."

I sat down heavily on the roller chair and tried to rein in my emotions. It would be very unprofessional to cry in front of a client, but I knew that this was going to end in euthanasia, and the very thought tore me up inside. Dr. Hanks was talking quietly with the owner as Winchester wandered around the aisle, oblivious to his situation. He was just enjoying the moment, exploring interesting things. That made it even worse, but I couldn't stop the thoughts from coming. He was so cute and innocent, and I just wanted to pick him up and hug him and tell him how sorry I was about his rotten luck.

Dr. Hanks' voice pulled me out of my spiral. "Justin, can you bring the x-ray cart inside for me?"

"Sure, of course." I was too far inside my feelings to consider it a strange request, and she held the door for me as I pushed the cart inside. Once we were in, it occurred to me that the cart didn't normally go inside, and I wasn't sure what I was supposed to be doing.

"I needed an excuse to talk to you in private," Dr. Hanks said. "I don't want to euthanize this goat. Would it be okay if

I asked her to sign ownership over to me? I'll amputate his leg, and he can come live at my house. I know we've done things like this in the past a few times, but I don't really know what the protocol is."

Seeing her trying to save the goat got me out of my funk and back into business mode. "That's definitely an option. But I have to warn you; this is how you start collecting animals, and it's a very slippery slope. You've got to be careful about which ones you take on or else you'll become a hoarder with way too many critters."

"I know," she said, nodding in agreement. "I've been planning to have a few goats for years, but I didn't have a place for them to live. Now that we're buying our farm, I'll have room for him... in a few months. I'll need to find a place for him to stay until we get moved, though. Maybe he can be a clinic goat for a while?"

That was the very instant that I knew that I was going to be a foster dad to a three-legged goat, and I felt an enormous sense of relief that he wasn't going to die over a broken leg. "I don't know if the clinic is the best place for him, but he can stay at our house. We have an empty stall he can live in, and our barn is safe for him to run around."

"Okay," she said. "I appreciate that. I can pay board for him."

"Don't be ridiculous!" I said. "Let's get a form signed and get him on the surgery schedule."

The owner was happy to turn over the goat instead of euthanizing him. Once that happened, things started to move quickly. The surgery was scheduled for the following day, and I debated about whether I wanted to watch it or not. I'm not very squeamish, so the blood and body parts didn't bother me. It was more the permanency of what was happening that made me uncomfortable. Once that leg was removed, that was it, no going back.

When I was newly sober, my mentor told me that he'd never met an alcoholic with a magazine subscription, because we all have this ridiculous fear of commitment. I thought that sounded a little far-fetched, and he was prone to exaggeration, but the more I get to know myself, the more I realize how right he was about that. I don't have any problem committing to a subscription because I can cancel it. My fear is with things that are permanent. People dying, body parts being removed, items being destroyed. You know, things that can't be undone. I didn't really understand this about myself until I got old enough that those things started happening in my life. Thank God for therapy!

The surgery went great. I will admit that I peeked through the window a few times just to see what was going on. With the doctor, tech, and vet student all standing around the operating table, I couldn't see anything, but the fact that they all looked calm and collected made me feel better. I chose to ignore the fact that when things are going poorly, it looks exactly the same. We see what we want to see, right?

The first thing we did when the goat recovered from anesthesia was discuss his name. Winchester just didn't seem right for him.

"I think it needs to reference the number three, somehow," I said. "It doesn't have to be right on the nose, like *Tripod*, but something clever and funny."

"Yeah," Dr. Hanks said. "Clever and funny, for sure." The rest of the team started throwing out ideas immediately.

"Triple Threat."

"Triple Crown."

"Scrambled Leggs."

"Hop Along."

"Little Tommy Triptych."

"Three Amigos."

"Scoot Scoot McGroot."

"Vincent van Goat."

"Billy the Kid."

"Wait!" I shouted. "Vincent van Goat. That was really good!"

"Vincent van Gogh cut his ear off, right?" Lexi asked.

"Yes, which is perfect," I said. "That gives the name multiple layers of apropos. It's three words, they both lost a body part, and there's a play on words. I love it!"

"All in favor of Vincent van Goat?" Dr. Hanks said. All the hands in the room went up. "It's unanimous!"

Vinnie stayed at the clinic for a few days after surgery, just to make sure everything was okay. And, with the matching turquoise leash and bandana around his neck, he was so stinking cute that no one could bear to be away from him for long, myself included. His eyes gleamed as he scampered around his stall, or the barn aisle, if there weren't any horses being worked on. He was the physical embodiment of pure joy, despite everything that had happened to him, or perhaps because of it. Instead of being despondent about his situation, he seemed to be living his life to the fullest extent possible. From sitting in laps to running laps, he was happy to be part of whatever was happening.

Friday morning came, and we had our weekly staff meeting. We sat in a circle in the aisleway, and Vinnie was working the crowd along with Tony, our clinic cat. Tony was after treats and ear scratches, while Vinnie was nibbling on coffee cups, straws, scrub tops, shoes, fingers, ink pens, donuts, and anything else that he could reach. Between the twelve of us in the circle, somewhere around a thousand pictures were taken.

"I think he's ready to go home with you guys," Dr. Hanks said. "His mobility has improved dramatically, and his incision looks great."

"But you have to bring him to the clinic every day so we can play with him," Lexi said. A chorus of agreement followed, and I laughed. Whether he wanted to be or not, Vinnie was already the Clinic Goat. Somehow, I didn't think he minded too much.

As expected, Vinnie's arrival at our farm caused a general uproar. He was going to live in the empty stall for a while, at least until his leg nub was completely healed. As I walked him down the barn aisle on the leash to his new home, the horses all stuck their heads out their stall doors, blowing and sniffing and snorting, staring at the wonder before them. Of course, they'd all been living with our sheep for years, and the next-door neighbors had goats, but as all horse people know, that didn't mean anything. This goat was new and different, and was most likely a lion or tiger in disguise, and was therefore terrifying.

On the opposite end of the interest spectrum, the dogs thought Vinnie was the most interesting thing they'd ever seen. Pookums, the shih tzu mob boss, immediately got in his face and explained that she was in charge of things. Leonard, the quintessential big dumb goofball mutt, was trying to lick every part of Vinnie at once, with an extra focus on his butt.

Vinnie handled the attention like a true professional.

He showed off his new sideways three-legged hop move a few times, and paid no particular attention to any of the snorting, whinnying, barking, and licking that was taking place. When we got to his stall, he immediately climbed on top of the flake of hay, plopped down in the middle of it, and started eating. I took his leash off and shooed the dogs out, closing the door behind me. The dogs set up a watch in front of the door, staring with rapt attention as the goat happily nibbled on interesting bits of hay.

I didn't get much work done the first few days Vinnie was there. I wanted him to get used to the dogs and horses, and get some exercise, so he got to run around the barn a lot under supervision. My other motive was to let the dogs get used to him being there so the novelty would wear off. Leonard was constantly licking him, and I was anxious to get past that stage. Vinnie mostly just tried to walk away from it, but once he realized that he could headbutt the dog, that could become a problem. After all, goats are goats, and dogs are dogs, and we all have instincts.

On Saturday afternoon, I made a discovery. Erica and I were sitting on the mounting block, watching Vinnie explore the yard. He was sniffing everything, but not actually eating anything. I moved him over to some delicious clover, and he gave it a sniff, but then wandered over to the tree and licked the bark.

"He doesn't know how to eat weeds," I said in amazement. "He knows about hay, but I don't think he ever learned that green plants are food."

"You may be right," Erica said. "There wasn't any green stuff at his old house, at least, not in the goat pen. This is probably the first time he's ever seen it up close."

I picked some clover and held it out to him. He sniffed it, and then bit my finger. "Hey!" I said, pulling my hand back. "You're not going to get any milk out of that. And you're focused on all the wrong stuff. We've got to teach you how to goat."

I spent the next ten minutes picking different weeds and leaves, presenting them one by one, but he didn't taste any of them. I tried sticking them in his mouth, but that didn't work. I rubbed leaf juice on my finger and let him suckle on it to get the taste, but it was all for nothing. He just didn't recognize any of it as food.

"Don't overdo it," Erica said after a while. "At some point, you're going to become as annoying to him as Leonard."

I laughed, and came back to sit beside her. "You're right. All things in moderation."

The one living plant Vinnie did seem to be fond of was the moss growing on the tree trunk in the front yard. As the days went by, that became his go-to spot. He didn't really nibble on it, he just licked it. A lot. Just to make sure I wasn't missing out on anything spectacular, I tried licking it too, but the appeal was lost on me.

As the days went by, Vinnie got more and more adept at getting around on three legs. He was learning how to run in brief spurts, and buck while running, and by the end of the first week, he was experimenting with climbing the mounting block. Going up wasn't a problem, it was coming down that flummoxed him. The first few times he crashed. Then he managed to go back down the two steps successfully, balancing on his front legs. I wasn't sure if it was on purpose or accidental, but it looked amazing! Of course, my phone was in my pocket when it happened, and once I was ready to video him, he didn't do it again, and instead moved on to something else.

While he didn't know what to do with green plants, Vinnie definitely knew what to do with hay. As I gave him more autonomy, he developed a routine. He would start at the stall next to his, where Cai had dribbled hay out her window. Once he had that cleaned up, he would go on to the next stall, and work his way around the inside of the barn. By the end of the second week, he had discovered the outside of the barn also had windows with hay dribbled everywhere. He was a committed clean-up crew of one. And with Leonard's interest in licking him waning, and the horses deciding that he wasn't going to eat them after all, he got to do it in relative peace.

By Vinnie's third week with us, he had the run of the farm during the day. At first, I tried to open his stall door and then feed the horses, but that quickly proved to be problematic. Vinnie couldn't figure out green plants, but somehow he understood that grain in a bucket was food, and he didn't care that it was for the horses.

The first day we did this, I learned that a twenty-pound goat can somehow exert a thousand pounds of downward force when determined to prevent me from removing him from the horse's breakfast. I had six buckets lined up on the feed room floor, five for the horses, and one for the donkeys. The feed was already meted out, and I was pulling up meds for Hannah Banana when Vinnie stuck his nose in the door.

"Hey, little buddy! You found me. What have you been up to?"

Vinnie bleated, and hopped forward a few steps into

the room. At this point, I was still focused on getting the meds together, and it hadn't occurred to me that he knew what feed in a bucket was about. A moment later, his head was in a bucket. Before I could even process that that was happening, his front feet were in the bucket, and his head was in the next bucket. He was scarfing down food like he hadn't eaten in days, rather than minutes.

"Whoa, whoa, whoa!" I put Hannah's pill and syringe on top of the feed can and attempted to pull Vinnie's head out of the bucket before he could do any more damage to the breakfast buffet. Somehow, he was stronger than me in that position, and I couldn't get his head out of the feed. We both strained, although he never missed a bite despite his exertion. It was like he was warping gravity, and his density had become that of a thousand-pound horse. I quickly switched tactics, as he was on track to eat a pound of ration balancer in less than thirty seconds. With one hand under his belly and the other under his chin, I heaved, and finally managed to lever him out of the feed buckets. Once he was in the air, his weight returned to normal, and I carried him back to his stall and put him down in front of his own flake of hay.

The next problem presented itself when I started bringing horses in. It hadn't really occurred to me that Vinnie had been spending his days standing in front of all these stall doors, eating hay spillage and watching the horses work on their big flakes. As a now-connoisseur of fine timothy hay, Vinnie knew an opportunity when he was presented with one, and as soon as I finished rolling the stall doors open and headed out to get horses, he was in Cai's stall, eating her hay for all he was worth. Cai spotted him before I did as we walked into the aisle, and she stopped short.

"What are you doing?" I asked, pulling on Cai and trying to manage Vespa, who was in my other hand and headed for her own stall. Cai snorted and pawed the floor once. I glanced in her door, and there was Vinnie, standing on top on her flake of hay.

There was no quick solution to that problem, so we went down the aisle and put Vespa in her stall first. With a free hand, I was able to scoop him up and deposit him outside the stall and get Cai inside, but it took a bit of doing. By the time I had Cai's halter off, Vinnie was in Ernie's stall eating his hay.

"You are turning into a giant pain in the butt," I told him. "I can already tell that you're going to have to stay in your house until everybody's in from now on." I set him down on his on flake of hay once again, and this time I closed the door. I might be a slow learner sometimes, but I get there eventually.

Once the rest of the crew were in their stalls, I let him back out. He didn't seem to hold a grudge about it, as he demanded a neck scratch before making a beeline to Cai's door to clean up her hay. She stuck her head out the door and watched him as she chewed, bits of hay raining down on him as he shot from one piece to the next.

After that experience, I did everything else first. Vinnie was horrified by this development, and stood at his door screaming at me the whole time. It's amazing how much noise a tiny goat can make. It's also amazing how the sound of a baby goat cry can cut right to my heart and make me feel like a horrible human. I think I might finally understand what other people experience when they hear a crying human baby. I don't know if it's the same, but this is as close as I've ever come to that.

For the first few days that week, I put Vinnie back in his stall when I had to go to the vet clinic or run errands. Otherwise, I left him to his own devices. I would go down every couple of hours to stretch my legs and make sure he wasn't wandering too far away, but he was never away from the barn. As long as there was a scrap of hay to be found, he was content to stay there looking for it.

Near the end of the third week, I decided to leave him out while I went to the bank and the recycle center. It was the next big step in having an autonomous three-legged barn goat. I felt confident that he wasn't going anywhere, and Leonard seemed to have lost interest in him all together. So, off I went. An hour later, my phone rang. It was Erica.

"Hey," I said. "What's up?"

"I can't find Vinnie."

"Are you at the house?" I asked. "I thought you had a full schedule today."

"I did," she said. "Ruth Ann canceled, so I brought the vet student over so we could take a look at Vinnie's incision and take an x-ray. Anyway, he's not in the barn, and I've wandered around all over the place looking for him. I thought maybe you took him to the clinic or something."

"No, but I did leave him out loose. Maybe he followed a butterfly into the woods. I'll be home in about twenty minutes or so, and I'll find him."

I was already kicking myself for leaving him out while I was gone. But if I had been there, working up at my computer, the same thing might have happened. I had been going two hours or more at a time without checking on him, and I hadn't even been gone that long yet. With a deep breath, I decided to quit beating myself up and just get home and find the goat.

Vinnie was nowhere to be found. I searched the barn, then ever-bigger circles around the barn and the trailer parking area. The pastures came next, and the riding arena. When he wasn't any of those places, I searched the barn again, in case he had come in while I was out looking for him. Finally, I started a grid-search of the woods. That took nearly an hour, but when I was done, I was convinced he wasn't there.

Where could he be? He was a goat, admittedly, but I felt confident that he hadn't made it past the fence anywhere. If he wasn't inside the fence, and he didn't go through it, that left two possibilities. Either someone came to the house and saw how adorable he was and stole him, which would likely be a delivery person, or someone came to the house, and he managed to get out the gate before it closed.

I went back down the driveway, which is three quarters of a mile, searching the ditches and accessible areas beside it. No Vinnie. I talked to the neighbors and showed them pictures in case he popped up in their yard. And then there was nothing else I could do. I went home and tried to get some work done while I waited for the phone to ring. It didn't ring.

When Erica got home, we went over every angle of the situation we could think of.

"Is there any place that you didn't look?" she asked.

"Well, I was looking for a live goat, so I didn't look inside the brambles in the back pasture, or inside some of those dense cedar clusters. I don't think he could get in there on three legs. But if we think something might have happened to him, that could be a different situation."

She sighed. "At this point, I think we have to consider the possibility that something happened to him. Wherever he is, he almost certainly didn't walk there."

"That's fair." I grabbed a flashlight off the counter. "It won't take long to check those places."

We started with the big cedar tree on the fence line. It was a dense mass of branches all the way to the ground. Sometimes one of the cats would hole up there, because it was nearly impenetrable, which made it a good fort for a cat. As soon as we got around behind the tree, I could see that something had been going on, as the pine needles and leaves were disturbed, and there were some gouges in the dirt.

I got on my hands and knees and crawled between the branches enough to get a look inside. I shined the light around, and a dark spot next to the trunk caught my eye. A ball of queasiness was forming in my belly as I wormed in closer and brushed the dead leaves away. It was Vinnie, and he was very clearly dead. A sob escaped my lips before I even knew it was there.

"Is he in there?" Erica called out. She sounded far away.

"Yeah, he's here." I forced the words out through my thickening throat. "He's dead."

I stuck the flashlight in my mouth and scooped up his little body. His head flopped in a way that told me his neck was broken, and I knew instantly there was only one way that could have happened, and him end up in here: Leonard. I used the building rage to extricate myself and Vinnie from under the tree. Once we were back out in the sunshine, Erica checked him over.

"His neck is broken," I said. My hands were shaking. "It had to be the dog. There's no way Vinnie walked all the way out here and broke his neck and then hid himself in there. I'm going to kill the dog. I'm going to shoot him until I run out of bullets, and then I'm going to beat him to death until I run out of rage. It's going to take a while."

"Let's focus on taking care of Vinnie," Erica said. "He's been dead for half the day now, so let's get him buried. Then we'll calm down and figure out what to do about Leonard."

I nodded mutely. We wrapped Vinnie in a towel, and I dug a hole with the tractor on the back fence where a lifetime of dogs and cats were buried. Leonard was right there with us, seemingly oblivious to what was happening other than exciting tractor stuff, which he loved. I wanted to kick him, or beat him to death with a stick, to somehow punish him for taking Vinnie away from us for no reason, to make him feel the pain I was feeling, to exact revenge on him for... for being a dog.

And that was the hell of it. Leonard was an apex predator. He might be docile most of the time, and have all his physical needs met by us, but at the end of the day, he still had instincts that drove a lot of his behavior. It was no different than one of the cats killing a baby rabbit, which happened once in a while. There was no need for food, but there was a base-level urge to chase something that registered as prey, and sometimes they were able to override that urge, and sometimes they weren't.

As I thought about the big picture of life on our farm, it finally registered that every day was a life and death struggle for everything on our farm except for the humans. The horses were constantly in fear of being killed by something, and while that was pretty unlikely, there were coyotes in the area that were technically predators, and an occasional bobcat. For everything smaller than a horse, whether it was one of our domesticated animals or a wild creature living in the woods beside the house, or even the mice and lizards in the barn and the snake in the scrap wood pile, they lived every moment in a very different world than the one Erica and I lived in. I was furious at Leonard for killing Vinnie, but was he wrong for the role he played, or was I wrong for expecting him to be something other than what he was?

I didn't acknowledge Leonard for two days. In my heart, I knew that I either had to forgive him, kill him, or find him a new home, because it wasn't fair to him for me to keep him without loving him. Once we were past the initial moment, there was no way I was going to kill him, as I'm not wired that way at all. I really didn't want to find a new home for him either, because he was a good dog 99% of the time, and I didn't want to risk him ending up in a bad situation, like the one we rescued him from to begin with. So, I settled on forgiveness. It just took two days for me to get it done.

I'd spent the better part of twelve years in therapy, trying to understand what drives my behavior and building tools to help me evolve past my instinctual, knee-jerk reactions. I'd made a lot of progress, to be sure, but I still failed to act the way I wanted to on a regular basis. If I could forgive myself for all those lapses, it would be hypocritical to deny Leonard one time, even if it was a big one. When I finally came to that conclusion, I was able to give him a hug and welcome him back into the family. It still hurt, but it was becoming a growth-hurt instead of a loss-hurt.

The four weeks that Vinnie spent in our lives were

wonderful. The death that we tried to spare him from with the surgery caught up to him anyway, but he had a tremendous impact on everyone in the vet clinic during that time. And his death taught me a few lessons and gave me a new perspective on things, so it wasn't meaningless. I hated that it happened, but I vowed to use the experience to somehow make my next effort at caring for an animal better for them. Now I know that instincts can overpower good sense and training. And I know that my experience is not the experience that our animals have, and while I tend to create these mental images of who they are, that's not reality. I have to accept them as they really are and protect them from one another. That's my responsibility. And for all they give me, that's the least I can give them.

14

The Case of the Vampire Real Estate Agent

While I work from home most of the time, I still end up riding around in the vet truck on a regular basis. And when you spend a lot of time driving around, you start to notice things, like real estate signs. Well, I do, anyway.

I first took notice of real estate signs when I sold my house in Georgia to move to Florida with Erica. The house down the street had a for-sale sign, and the agent looked like a glamour model from the 1980's, big hair, dark eyes, the whole thing. Despite all my efforts to evolve, I'm still a man, and on some instinctual level, I guess I respond to such things, because I called her.

The woman I met shared little resemblance to the

picture on the sign, and I realized that it looked like a picture from the '80's because it *was* a picture from the '80's. She just hadn't updated it in thirty years. I guess if it ain't broke, don't fix it, right? But she sold my house, so that was the important thing.

Anyway, back to north Florida. The woman on the signs I kept seeing definitely drew my attention, but not because she was attractive. It's not that she was unattractive, with her flawless pale white skin, nearly-white blonde hair, and blood-red lipstick. It was the way she seemed to be trying to look like an attractive woman, or maybe just look like a human, period, but not quite pulling it off. I have a very active imagination, I know, but this person was clearly a vampire.

Once I figured out that she was a vampire, I couldn't *not* see it. And she had signs everywhere, big plywood signs on country properties, so her picture was huge. At my core, I'm a writer, and I make up stories, and this was just too good to ignore. Fortunately, Erica is a good sport about such things.

"There she is," I said one day, slowing to point at a sign. "That's the one."

"Oh, for sure," Erica said, glancing at it. "Definitely a vampire."

"Right? There's not a particular thing that signals it, but you still know."

"So how is there a picture of her? I thought vampires didn't show up in pictures and reflections and such."

This is the magic of creating a story that I love so much. It's not just dreaming up the story itself, it's the series of logic problems you have to solve along the way. Problem number one: How is there a picture of a vampire?

"Well, there are a couple of possibilities that come to

mind," I said. "It could be a body double. I've seen movies where the vampires have a human proxy that looks like them that handles things in the daytime. Or maybe vampires didn't show up in old school photos, but digital cameras can capture them."

"I think the people that made up the vampire rules didn't know much about actual vampires," Erica said. "As we learned from *Twilight,* vampires can be out in the daytime. Who knows what else they were wrong about?"

"Fair point," I said. "If you have a proxy doing the daytime stuff, being a real estate agent seems like a lot of work and unnecessary publicity for your cover persona. Maybe it's really her."

"Even if the vampire is doing all that herself, why be such a visible figure, like you said?"

I shrugged. "Well, it's a great way to meet people, you learn a lot about them in a short time, and if they don't have close family and disappear during a transition from one town to another, who would ever suspect the real estate agent? Seems like a good way to keep yourself in business as a vampire."

"There's the issue of her name," Erica said. "*Darcy LeMont.* Darcy is probably short for Druscilla or something. I don't think she's trying very hard to hide her vampiness."

"She's leaning into it," I said. "People like edgy things, so maybe she decided to just market herself as a vampire real estate agent. It's a niche thing, but that's how you make it these days. You have to find your target market and give them what they want. I kinda like it! She's scary as hell, but I'd still buy a house from her. You know, in the daytime. In a crowded place with lots of witnesses."

As time went on, we added layer after layer to the story. It became a game for us, building a complex persona around the picture on the signs. For example, we passed one of the signs one night after dark.

"Did you see that?" I asked, looking vainly in the mirror, trying to get a glimpse of the sign.

"See what?" Erica glanced up from her phone.

"The vampire lady wasn't on the sign. I could read the text, but I couldn't see her picture."

"Well, it *is* dark," Erica said. "Maybe that has something to do with it."

"Exactly. At sunset, she came down from the sign and went to hunt. She could be anywhere." It occurred to me as I said it that we were on a dark, two-lane road in the middle of nowhere, and there wasn't another car in sight. This was the exact scenario that every vampire story in the history of vampire stories used. "I may have just given myself the heebie-jeebies. If we see a blonde chick standing in the middle of the road, I'm going to floor it."

"I don't think she qualifies as a chick," Erica said. "If she's three hundred years old, she's aged out of the chick category."

"I don't think you're taking our situation very seriously. Our lives may be in jeopardy this very moment."

It was fun. And for months and months, a story was all it was. Then one day we had an emergency call, and everything changed.

It actually started an hour before the emergency call came in. Erica and I were at a farm in High Springs to check out a new foal and run an IgG, or immunoglobulin test. This particular foal was quite healthy and energetic. He also didn't like having his temperature taken, which isn't unusual, and he stomped on my foot as I tried to hold him for Erica. Foals aren't particularly heavy at one day old, but their hooves are very small and pointy, and he got me right on the arch. It wasn't a serious injury, but I was limping a little.

On the way home from that visit, Erica's phone rang.

"Hello, Dr. Lacher."

"This is Doris Flint. Can you hear me?" The voice coming over the car speakers was elderly, and very weak. It reminded me of my grandmother, who had a very hard time projecting her voice enough to be heard. My uncle used to joke that she had used up all of her loud voice yelling at him when he was a kid. Naturally, I formed an image of her as the lady on the phone did her best to explain the situation.

"Yep, I've got you," Erica said, turning up the volume. "What can I do for you?"

Doris cleared her throat. "I'm not able to get out of my house right now. I'm having some health problems. But I've got two horses in the pasture. Hold on." She moved the phone away, but we could hear her coughing. "I'm sorry. My throat gets dry. I don't talk very much these days. What was I saying?"

"You said you've got two horses in the pasture," Erica said. She had the laptop open and was typing as she spoke. "It looks like we've seen you once before, several years ago. You've got Ringo and Short Stuff, right?"

"Yes, that's right. I can usually see them grazing up by the house in the mornings, and they go back in the trees in the evenings." She paused to cough again. "Ringo was laying down when I looked out this morning. I forgot about it when my home health nurse came, but I looked out the window again this evening when I came in to get some soup, and he's still laying there. I think something must be wrong."

Erica pointed to the left as we approached an intersection, and I put the turn signal on. "We're about fifteen minutes away from you right now, but we're headed your direction, okay? We'll take a look at Ringo and see what's going on. Do you want me to call you, or come to the door? I can do either one."

"I'm sitting in my chair," Doris said. "I leave the door unlocked in case the ambulance has to come get me again. You can just come in."

"Okay. We'll see what's going on with Ringo, and then I'll come in and talk to you."

Erica wrapped up the call and pointed to the right as we approached another intersection. It was closing in on dusk, and I drove as fast as I dared, trying to get us there before we lost the light.

"It looks like Dr. Simpson saw this horse once for a laceration six years ago. I've never been there."

"How old is he?" I asked. "I'm guessing he hasn't been vaccinated in a long time. Being down all day could be a lot of different things, and none of them good. Colic, encephalitis, broken leg, abscess..."

"He's thirty-three," Erica said. "If he hasn't moved all day, or maybe longer, he might not even be alive. If he *is* alive, he's going to be severely dehydrated. And at that age, this isn't going to be good. Turn left up here, and then it should be the third driveway down on the right."

As soon as we turned the corner, I knew where we were. This area was being developed, and the few remaining farm properties were for sale, and would soon be in the middle of town. Urban sprawl had to be a hard thing to deal with for the people who had been out in the country and were now being surrounded by neighborhoods. Doris was one of those people, and the picture on the for-sale sign by her mailbox was none other than my favorite vampire real estate agent.

I suppressed a shiver as we pulled into the driveway. It wasn't dark yet, so Darcy was still on the sign, but the sun would be down in the next half an hour. We were here for an emergency, so I tried to put the vampire story in the back of my mind and focus on reality, but it was hard. It was *really* hard. And in retrospect, I'm not sure I actually tried that much.

The driveway ended next to an old farmhouse. It was in a state of disrepair, but it had clearly been a cute place in years past. The banisters leading up to the covered porch were old wagon wheels, flanked by crumbling flower boxes filled with weeds. A porch swing hung by one chain, the other end dangling next to an old rusty milk can.

In front of us, a small barn sat just inside a barbed wire fence. I could guess how the horse had gotten lacerated six years prior. Barbed wire was an endless source of emergencies for us, and something that Erica preached about constantly. Off to the left, partially obscured by the tall weeds growing through the fence, a black horse lay flat out. I grabbed the stethoscope and thermometer and we headed for the gate. My foot was still sore from where the foal got me, but I powered through it.

Before we even got inside the pasture, it became clear that the horse was dead, and had been for a while. The upper legs were sticking straight out, and his abdomen was swollen significantly. The buzz of flies grew louder as we approached.

"I think we probably needed to be here yesterday," I said. "I'm surprised the vultures haven't found him yet."

Erica walked around Ringo, looking him over. "I don't see anything that tells me what went down. But yeah, I think this probably happened last night or this morning. Poor guy."

I glanced around. "There's supposed to be another one here, right?"

She nodded. "Yeah, Short Stuff. He's a mini. Let's go talk to Doris, and then we'll come see if we can get eyes on him before it gets dark."

We turned back to the gate and made our way to the house. The more I walked, the more my foot was throbbing, and I started to wonder if I had a broken bone or something. Erica knocked on the door and opened it slowly.

"Doris? It's Dr. Lacher, the veterinarian."

I followed her into a living room that probably hadn't changed much since the 1960's. The flowered wallpaper was hidden by framed black and white photos of people in suits and dresses, and the room was dominated by a huge console television in a beautiful wood frame, with two foil-wrapped antennas sticking out the top. A smaller, and much newer, television sat on top of it. There were knick-knacks everywhere, tiny porcelain figurines of swans and angels and horses. It was so similar to my grandma's house that I felt like I had stepped into a time machine.

Doris sat in an old rocking chair under a lamp. A TV tray beside the chair was stacked with books, magazines, and a big beige phone, another element from my grandma's house in my childhood. She was tiny and frail, and I hated that she was about to get the bad news about her horse.

"I thought that might be the real estate agent," Doris

said. "She's supposed to come by at seven to set some rat traps for me."

It took a second for me to process what she'd said. Darcy LeMont was on her way here! Right now! This couldn't happen. I was in such a state of shock that I almost missed her next words.

"I reckon Ringo's dead," she went on, her soft voice displaying the resolve of someone who has come to terms with her situation.

Erica nodded. "Yes, he is. I couldn't see any obvious reasons, but the computer says he's in his thirties, so it could be any number of things."

Doris nodded, looking down at her lap. "It's probably best that he's gone. I'm trying to sell this place before I end up in hospice, and nobody wants to take on an old horse. Did you see Shorty out there?"

"No, I was going to ask you if he's still here. We'll go make sure he's okay before we leave. Do you want me to arrange for someone to come bury Ringo?"

"Yes, please do." Doris stopped and coughed. It was a dry cough, but it still looked painful, and I felt bad for her. "And if you know anyone who would take a thirty-something year-old mini gelding, I've got to figure out a plan for him, too. Is it wrong to just put him to sleep? He's lived out there with Ringo since Ronald Reagan was president. He's never even left the property."

"I don't think that's unreasonable," Erica said. "But I might have a place where he can live in a field with another old guy that just lost his buddy. I can check on that tomorrow."

We headed back out to the barn, and I stopped at the

truck and grabbed a flashlight. The sun was dropping below the tree line, and the back half of the pasture was heavily wooded. Since Short Stuff was nowhere to be seen, it stood to reason that he was holed up back in there somewhere. I hoped it was a short search, as my foot was not happy with all the activity.

"Did you catch the part where the vampire is on her way here to set rat traps?" I asked, swinging the gate closed behind Erica. "This is a disaster of epic proportion unfolding in real time."

"I did catch that," Erica said. "But why is it a disaster?"

The line between the story and reality was too thin for me to see, and I was on the verge of a panic attack. "Are you kidding me? One look at me, and she'll know that I know she's a vampire. And I doubt that she'll be kind enough to turn me into a vampire rather than killing me. And she obviously killed the horse, and is coming back to finish off the rest of the occupants here. First Ringo, then the rats, Shorty, Doris, and now us. We have to get out of here!"

Erica burst into laughter. "I'll grant you that she should never meet you, because I don't think you could avoid making it extremely weird and uncomfortable for everyone. Let's go find Shorty before it gets pitch black in there."

"That's another thing," I said, turning on my light and limping toward the trees. "I think that foal broke my foot. The vampire will definitely sense that I'm injured. She's coming here to hunt, and I'm stumbling around in the dark with a bum foot. I might as well hang a sign around my neck asking her to take me out."

"Maybe she'll let you be a minion and eat bugs," Erica said with a grin. "That's something to hope for, right?"

We split up and began working our way to the back of the field. It was a long skinny property, so Erica and I weren't too far apart, but I couldn't tell how far back it went. Once we were in the trees, it was slow going. There were a million places a mini could hide, even if he wasn't trying. I swung the light around in a slow arc, calling for him every few steps, as Erica did the same thing on her side. My foot was announcing its displeasure with every step, but it seemed to have leveled out instead of getting even worse. It was a small thing, but with the looming threat of facing an all-powerful creature of the night and fighting for my life, I was grateful for it.

Short Stuff was all the way against the back fence line. I had just about decided that he must be dead already too, when my light picked up a white blaze. He was a tall mini, nearly pony size, chestnut with a mostly white face. His mane was massive and stuck straight up. When the light hit him, he knickered and trotted over to me.

"Oh, now you come running?" I said, patting him on the neck. "You must be deaf as a post. Or maybe you're just a mini, and you like making people walk all the way out here." I thought for a moment. "Or, you saw the vampire drain Ringo, and you were hiding from her, but you realized that I'm one of the good guys and you want me to save you."

Erica made her way over and gave Shorty a quick inspection. "He seems fine."

"I think so, too. Now, let's get out of here while we still can. It's ten minutes 'til seven."

Erica laughed. "You're a mess. I think it's hilarious that you've got yourself worked up into a tizzy over this lady."

"There's a tiny part of me that will admit that she might

not be a vampire, but it's a very small part, and it's been wrong about things before."

"Alright, hush up about it for a minute so I can call Ed to come bury Ringo."

I hobbled back to the barn in silence as Erica talked on the phone. I knew I was being ridiculous, but I was too deep in it to get back to the surface. And honestly, this was the most exciting thing I had experienced in forever, and I was loving every second of it. But the thought of coming face to face with Darcy was terrifying, regardless of whether she was a vampire or just a nice lady who was trying to sell a house. Erica was right. There was no way I could get through that without making a complete ass out of myself. My urgency to get out of there was justified.

Back in the living room, Erica was wrapping things up with Doris.

"Short Stuff looks fine. We found him all the way in the back. I'd rather see if I can get him to a new home as a companion, since they're about the same age, and both relatively healthy."

Doris nodded, and began rummaging through the pile of stuff beside the chair. "I'd like that, too, very much. Thank you for doing all this. How much is the bill?"

Erica waved her hand. "There's no bill. We didn't really do anything. Save your money for Ed. He's on his way over now to bury Ringo for you. Is there a particular place you want him put to rest?"

Doris sighed. "He loved standing in the shade under that big live oak behind the barn. But this is all probably going to get turned into a shopping center or something, so I don't guess it really matters, does it? Isn't that sad? I've lived in this house since 1968, back when that was a dirt road out front, and it was a twenty-minute drive to the nearest store." She was hit with another coughing fit, so we made our goodbyes and returned to the truck.

The dash clock said it was 7:01 when I started the engine, and my sense of urgency redoubled. I turned around and headed up the driveway. When we got to the pavement, there was a car approaching, so I waited. It began to slow, and the turn signal came on.

"Oh no, that's her!" I screamed. The vet truck surged out onto the pavement, tires squealing as I floored the gas pedal, and we shot past the red SUV as it began to turn into the driveway. I couldn't see in the window as we passed, but there was a big sticker on the door identifying it as a real estate agent vehicle. My heart was hammering in my chest, and my hands were squeezing the wheel hard enough to make my knuckles hurt. "Oh my God, that was so close! That was way too close! Holy crap!"

"Um, Justin, you're doing seventy in a forty-five, and you're going the wrong way."

I pried my eyes away from the rearview mirror and glanced at Erica. "What?"

"Home," she replied calmly, pointing the other way. "We're supposed to be going home."

I slowly came to my senses. My muscles were saturated with adrenaline, and I felt heavy and sluggish. At the same time, I was exhilarated in a way that I'd never felt before. What a rush! What an absolutely insane experience that whole thing had just been! I got the truck slowed down a bit and started looking for a place to turn around.

"Yeah, of course," I said at last. "I've got this. Nothing

to worry about."

I still felt a tingle of electricity up my spine when we drove back past Doris's driveway, but nothing happened. Apparently, the vampire was going to save us for another day.

15

Lights, Camera, Action!

There are a lot of fringe benefits that come with being married to Erica. For one, she knows thousands of people, so if I need an expert of any kind, she can probably connect me to one. This has worked out in some surprising ways. For example: early on, I was having some problems with the audio during our monthly live seminar. I could make it sound great for the live audience, but the people watching on Facebook and YouTube couldn't hear. And when I got it to where it was good online, the live audience couldn't hear. Erica introduced me to one of her clients who knows audio production inside and out, and he helped me figure out the problem and find a solution. Over the years since, he's taught me a ton of stuff, and turned out to be a good friend.

One neat thing that I never expected was getting to meet a lot of really high achievers, people who are at the top of their game. A lot of this has come along with having a successful podcast. We've been able to interview some amazing people who are doing the work that is moving equine medicine to the next level. From equine genetics researchers to the PhD advisors who write the books on equine nutrition to the leading experts on the gut microbiome, talking to the people who are the most knowledgeable in the world on their subject is an amazing and humbling experience. Outside of the podcast, I've also gotten to meet some top-level riders and trainers. One of our clients has a horse that's in the running to be selected for the U.S. Olympic Dressage team, and I've met several Olympic-level Eventers. Being able to stand near those people and be inspired by their passion and dedication is something I never encountered before I met Erica, and it makes me feel like I can do more.

Another thing I never dreamed I'd do in a million years was be a videographer in a surgery suite. In Book 2 of this series, I talked about Erica's horse, Ernie, and his colic surgery. I got to be in the OR for that and filmed a lot of it on my phone. Since then, I've really gotten into video production, and I now have a full broadcast and recording studio. And because Erica has a great relationship with the surgeons at the referral hospital in Ocala, I've been able to go back there with video cameras and lights and film a variety of surgeries on horses, and THAT'S a cool experience!

The first surgery I attended was a plantar fasciotomy and neurectomy. I was super excited to film it, and it wasn't until the night before as I was piling all my camera gear on the kitchen floor that I realized I didn't even know what it was. Erica was sitting at the table responding to emails and raised her eyebrows as I paused and glanced over at her.

"So, this is probably going to sound silly, but what is a plant... planter..." I grabbed the envelope off my desk and looked at my notes. "Plantar fasciotomy and neurectomy? Am I saying that right?"

"Yeah, mostly. It's actually two different things. The fasciotomy means they're going to cut the fascia around a swollen ligament. Plantar tells you which part of the body it's in, which for people would be the foot, and for horses it's the lower leg. And the neurectomy is just cutting a nerve so the horse can't feel pain in a particular spot."

"Wow, that seems bad," I said. "Is it permanent?"

Erica laughed. "It's not bad, and no, it's not permanent. But this horse has a problem in his leg, and when that happens, they tend to rest that leg a lot, and adjust the way they move, and that can cause a whole load of other problems in the other legs and feet. The nerve will grow back in a few months, but hopefully by then the other problem, which is probably a swollen suspensory ligament, will be resolved."

"Ah, that makes sense."

The next morning, I got up at 4:30 a.m. so I could get the horses in and fed and make it to Ocala by 7:00 a.m. The surgery wouldn't actually start until nine, but I wanted to capture the entire process. As a chronic over-preparer, I'd loaded everything I had in terms of gear, just so there was no chance that I'd forget something. I probably wouldn't use most of it, but chance favors a prepared mind, and I have a very low risk tolerance.

When I arrived, the surgery techs were walking the horse out of his stall. It was just beginning to get light outside, and I hurried to get my gear unloaded. I decided to leave some of it in the truck, as I was already missing the first steps. I piled the rest in the corner just inside the surgery suite door and quickly put a camera on the tripod and went to find the crew.

"Good morning!" I called out, poking my head in the door to the prep room. "I'm Justin Long. Hopefully someone told you I was coming."

"Hi, Justin, I'm Nancy, the head surgery tech. Dr. Munns said you were going to be videoing this morning, right?"

"Right. I remember you, by the way. You were here last year when my wife's horse had colic surgery."

"I was! Ernie, right? How is he?"

I was impressed that she remembered his name. It had taken me a month of living with him to get it memorized. "He's doing pretty good. Retirement has been a good thing for him."

She smiled. "That's good. We're just about to drop this guy and get him on the table so we can start prepping. I'm not sure what all you're trying to video. Is it just the surgery?"

"No, I was hoping to get the whole thing, if that's okay. I probably won't use a lot of it, but the more footage I can get, the better. Just tell me where I can be that won't be in your way. I don't want to interfere with anything."

"That's fine," she said. "We're going to take him in the induction room as soon as Keith gets all his vitals, and we'll get him sedated. I'll have to keep you on the outside of the room for that part, just to keep you safe, but once he's down, you can start filming."

"That's fine, I understand. And I'm giving you

permission right now to yell at me and tell me to get out of the way if I'm in a bad spot. But hopefully it won't be necessary!"

"Don't worry," Keith said from the other side of the horse. "Nancy never passes on an opportunity to yell at people."

"Hey, get back to work over there!" Nancy laughed and turned back to me. "We have a good time here, and you'll be fine. I'll show you where the sterile fields are, and as long as you stay away from those, you're good. The interns will be here soon, and they like to blast music, so it might get loud. I hope that won't mess up your video."

"No, I'm not recording audio at all. I'll do a voiceover later. I remember the music from Ernie's surgery, it was pretty rowdy." I smiled at the memory. If you didn't have a personal relationship with the horse on the table, it was a lot easier to relax and have a good time while doing your job, and that's the frame of mind you want to keep the doctors in. A stressed-out surgeon is the last thing you need! As I had learned then, loud music and jokes were part of how they made that happen.

Keith directed me to the changing room where I put on a scrub top and pants, a hair net and hat, crocs, and a face mask. I berated myself for not showing up even earlier to get my gear set up and change clothes, as I was missing out on the action. I threw my street clothes in a locker and raced back down the hall.

There was a small window in the door to the induction room, but it was far too scratched up and cloudy to film through. I watched as Dr. Sanders, one of the interns, gave the horse a shot, then got him up against the wall. Keith swung a padded panel out from the adjoining wall, creating a stall of sorts around the horse. The techs pushed on the panel, keeping the horse up against the wall, and Dr. Sanders managed his head. A minute later, he sat back on his haunches, and slowly crumpled to the floor.

Up until that point, everything had been happening at a calm, seemingly leisurely pace. As soon as the horse was out, everyone went into high gear. I grabbed my camera and set up in the corner out of the way as Keith opened the doors and rolled the surgery table over. The horse was already on his side, and Nancy was placing yellow straps at his feet. It took me a minute to get all the settings right on the camera, but I hit the record button just in time to capture Dr. Sanders placing a catheter in the horse's neck. She sutured it in place, and I zoomed back a bit to get all the activity.

At some point while I was focused on Dr. Sanders and the catheter, another intern, Dr. DuVal, had arrived with a breathing tube. As soon as the catheter was done, she began feeding it into the horse's mouth. It looked awfully big to me, but then, horses need a lot of air, so there's that. A moment later, Keith powered up the overhead crane and dropped the hook over the horse. It was the same kind of crane that was in the mechanic shop I had worked in during a previous lifetime, and I wondered, just for a second, if the people that built them had any idea what all they got used for.

There was a yellow strap on each foot, and as soon as the hook was down, they slid the straps over the hook and began lifting him up. There were more and more things happening simultaneously by then, and I had to pick what I was going to record and let the rest go. Every time I looked away from the horse, I would see a new person in the room that hadn't been there before. One was rolling a shop vac across the floor, while another had a cart loaded down with clippers, scrub, and gauze squares.

The interns and techs guided the horse through the air and down onto the surgery table. As soon as he touched down, the people on the sides grabbed the pads off the floor and installed them on the siderails to hold him upright on his back, while Dr. DuVal managed his head and began hooking up the ventilator to the tube sticking out of his mouth. The straps came off the hook, and they rolled the table to the center of the floor. I took the camera off the tripod and did a slow circle around everything, walking in an exaggerated crouch to keep the camera steady. It was the first time I had filmed anything with this many moving parts, and it was a challenge to maintain awareness of what was happening around me and still keep the camera pointed at the action.

While the doctors were working on attaching all the life support equipment up front, the techs began clipping all the hair off the leg that was getting the procedure. There were two sets of clippers going at the same time, while a third person ran the shop vac hose and sucked up all the hair. They had obviously done this process as a team many times before, and it was like watching a ballet. The clippers started at the top, side by side, and worked their way down together, while the hose went back and forth beneath them, catching the hair before it could fall. I made a mental note to try that the next time we clipped a horse at home. Getting a mountain of hair off the mats on our wash rack was next to impossible. Of course, convincing a horse that the clippers and the shop vac are both acceptable things could be another problem altogether.

The clipping process lost its initial excitement, and I moved up front to see what the interns were doing. There were a number of wires, tubes, and hoses hanging off the cart by his head. I recognized the anesthesia machine from Ernie's surgery, but I didn't know what anything else was.

"Can you tell me what some of this stuff does?" I asked.

Dr. DuVal smiled. Well, the corners of her eyes crinkled, which was all I could see between her mask and her hat. "Sure! The ventilator pumps air through this tube and breathes for the horse, because they forget to do that for themselves once they're under. The anesthesia gas goes through there too, and that's what keeps him asleep. The IV drip delivers some other drugs through the catheter, which is what Dr. Sanders is connecting now. The rest of this equipment monitors his vitals. We're tracking heart rate, blood pressure, CO2 output, temperature, all kinds of stuff. That way we can tell how he's doing, and if we need to adjust any of the drugs during the process."

"Very cool," I said. "What are some of the big things you're watching for during surgery?"

"Waking up!" the interns said in unison, then burst out laughing.

"Does that happen a lot?"

Dr. DuVal shook her head. "No, not actually waking up. But you want to keep them pretty close to it. If you over-anesthetize, you risk them dying on the table, so you want to keep them closer to awake than too deep asleep. If you let them get too awake, they start to move, and that's what the surgeons freak out about. But different horses metabolize the drugs at different rates, just like people, so you have to watch it constantly and make adjustments on the fly."

"Are you both doing that on this surgery?" I asked.

"No, Dr. Sanders is on surgery, and I'm on anesthesia today."

"Okay, thanks for the info," I said. "I'll let you get back to it."

"No problem," Dr. DuVal said. "Make sure you spell my name right in the credits!"

I laughed, and stepped back, putting the camera back on the tripod. The techs had finished clipping the leg and were now scrubbing in earnest. They had worked the chlorhexidine into a thick lather with small brushes, and were alternating between cleaning and rinsing with alcohol, which also included washing the brushes out each time. This process went on, back and forth, and I began to understand that preparing the horse for surgery was a much longer and more tedious process than the surgery itself. After a while, I shut the camera off and let it charge. You can only use so much cleaning and scrubbing footage.

The scrub took forever, and I got bored. I was wandering around the room, looking at all the various equipment, when a person in scrubs came out of the surgery suite. She rolled the big door open, and I took that as a sign that we were getting close.

"Can I go ahead and set up some lights and a camera in here?" I asked.

She shrugged. "I guess. I'm just an extern."

I decided to go for it. Nancy was there to keep me in line, so I kept an ear out for her voice as I set up lights and tripods and carried them in the open door. No admonishment came. When I got everything arranged, I went back out to check on the scrubbing progress. They had a towel draped around the leg, so I got beside the camera and waited for something to happen.

A voice rang out across the room. "Doctors are scrubbing, final scrub!"

I glanced around, looking for the source of the announcement, and realized that Dr. Sanders was nowhere to be seen. If she was shadowing the surgeon, it made sense that she would be in the scrub room, and I knew from Ernie's colic surgery that it takes a long time for the people to scrub in, too. It's almost as bad as the horse, but with less hair removal.

"Alright everybody!" Nancy shouted. "One minute to move, let's get everyone on the table."

I turned the camera on and took it off the tripod. I was starting to wish I had a gimbal, which is a tool that holds the camera steady when you're making moving shots. Everything I had done prior to this had been on a tripod, but filming a surgery was different in every way from what we did at home. Following the horse on the surgery table as they pushed him from the prep room to the operating room would be a great shot if I could hold the camera steady enough. I positioned myself near the head of the table and hit the record button.

Nancy made sure everyone was in place and gave the order. "Three, two, one, push!"

They got the table rolling and moved past me, with a tech pushing the cart holding the ventilator and anesthesia monitors keeping pace beside them. I pivoted slowly as they came by, trying to zoom out smoothly as they filled my screen, then fell in behind them as they went through the wide doorway into the operating room. Halfway across the floor, they began to reverse their effort and slow the table and steered it to a gentle stop under the big surgery lights hanging from the ceiling.

As soon as they had it in place, Keith lowered another overhead crane, and quickly attached a strap to the leg that was to be operated on and hoisted it up a bit. While he was doing that, Nancy put long, skinny plastic bags over each of the other feet and pulled them down to cover the legs.

I made my way around them in a slow circle, trying not to be in the way while filming the action. The overhead lights were brighter in here, and once I completed a circuit, I stopped to make some adjustments on the camera and put it on the other tripod. I had just gotten it going again when another door burst open to my left, and a doctor came bustling in, pushing a large table piled with surgery packs and sheets.

"Good morning, everyone, good morning, good morning! It's a fine day to be alive, and a fine day to make cinematic history. Who's ready to do some surgery?"

His energy and enthusiasm spread through the room, and a chorus of greetings and cheers were returned. I kept the camera trained on him as he moved across the space and parked the table beside the horse. When it was in place, he came over and gave me an elbow bump in greeting.

"Hey, Justin! Glad you made it."

"Good morning, Dr. Hotchkiss," I said. "Thanks again for doing this."

"No problem at all. Do you have everything you need? Is there anything you want me to do while you're recording? My Dr. Frankenstein quotes are a solid ten, and I do a passable Fred Astaire dance routine, but I'm rusty."

"Who is Fred Astaire?" Keith asked, dropping a wink in

my direction. "Was he on *American Idol* or something?"

I laughed. "I'm all set. I won't interfere with you at all during the surgery. Just pretend like I'm not here. I'll move around if I need a better angle or something. Are the extra lights going to bother you?"

He stepped over beside the horse and did a slow turn. "No, not at all. If anything, it will probably make it even better. My left side is my best side, by the way. If you shoot from over there, you can really capture the twinkle in my eye."

"I'll keep that in mind," I said with a chuckle.

Keith and Nancy were by the table waiting for him. As soon as he turned back, they began to drape the horse in big blue sterile sheets. Soon, the only thing visible of the horse was his head and the exposed leg. Dr. Hotchkiss began laying out instruments on the table while the techs finished getting the sheets affixed.

"Okay, let's do a final scrub on this leg," Dr. Hotchkiss said. "I'm going to do a glove change, and we'll get going. Nancy, do we have the PRP and the ultrasound ready?"

"It's all set to go," Nancy said. "I just have to roll it over when you're ready."

"We'll inject that first, then I'll open him up and do the neurectomy, and strip some fascia away. Back in a minute."

Keith and Nancy scrubbed the exposed leg again. I couldn't believe how much effort went in to cleaning the area, even though I knew that horses were perpetually dirty. I got some video of Dr. DuVal as she checked the horse's blink response and wrote his vitals on the chart, then went back to talk to Keith.

"I'm pretty sure you've been scrubbing this leg for at

least an hour," I said. "The alcohol gauze looks clean to me. How do you know when it's enough?"

"The first half of the scrub is about removing dirt," he said. "After that, it's about reducing the bacteria load. Say there's a billion bacteria on his skin in this area. If we can kill half of them, then that reduces his infection risk by fifty percent. You can't get them all, but the more you get, the better."

"Oh, I get it," I said. "I wasn't thinking about that part of things."

"It's really important," Nancy said. "They have all kinds of bacteria on their skin, and viruses, and fungus, and God knows what. You don't want that stuff getting inside the incision. That's why the surgeon put the suture that he's going to close it up with in an antibacterial solution to soak." She pointed to the table where a shallow pan was filled with needles and thread in a clear liquid.

Before I could respond, the door burst open again, and Dr. Hotchkiss and Dr. Sanders came in, holding their hands up in front of them and very pointedly not touching anything. I slipped back over by the tripod and got ready as Nancy rolled the ultrasound machine over.

"Alright, folks, let's play some music and get this party started!" Dr. Hotchkiss did a shuffle step and picked up the ultrasound probe. Dr. DuVal turned the stereo on, and the room was immediately flooded with pop music. It was funny to me that Dr. Hotchkiss, who had to be close to fifty, was jamming to the likes of Pink and Taylor Swift. I decided the never-ending rotation of recently graduated interns working under him probably kept him plugged into the current music scene. I admired his openness to it and made a mental note to work on my own attitude about such things.

I shifted the camera closer once they were in position, so that it was looking over the doctor's shoulder. His headlamp was intensely bright, and I had to adjust the settings again. It was almost like shooting outside in full sunlight. I grabbed the second camera from behind me and aimed it at the ultrasound machine. I was close, but not too close, and looked to Nancy for approval. She caught my questioning glance and gave me a nod. Fortunately, that position had me close enough to hear the surgeon as he talked to Dr. Sanders, despite the music.

"Okay, we're going to put some sterile lube on the probe and put it right up here on the suspensory ligament. I want to make sure I can see the screen, and still keep an eye on my needle so I can keep it straight without moving my head a lot. It's a technique you just have to keep refining until it becomes a habit. So, I can see the ligament there, and that lesion is right in the middle, and that's the source of all our problems here. I want to get the PRP right in the middle of it. You can see the needle on the ultrasound there."

I glanced at the ultrasound screen. There was a circle in the middle of a line, which I guessed was the lesion on the ligament, but I didn't really know. But as he inserted the needle, I could see it moving sideways across the screen. I desperately hoped the second camera was picking it up clearly. With that thought, I turned on the microphone. I wouldn't be able to use the audio with the music in the background, but if I could capture what he was saying, it would be useful when I scripted the narration, and maybe reduce the number of questions I'd have to ask Erica.

"Okay, once we're at the lesion, I'm just going to move

the probe some and get it from another angle. Always remember that this is 2D, and we're working in 3D. You want to verify your needle placement from a cross-angle before you push the plunger."

The static on the ultrasound screen shifted, and I lost the ability to make sense of any of it. I returned my focus to the camera, and tried to remember that I was there to record the event, not gawk at what was happening. It was hard, though, because it was so interesting, especially with Dr. Hotchkiss teaching the intern. He was a very engaging person.

"Okay, PRP is in. What's the next step?"

"Make the incision," Dr. Sanders said.

"That's right." He pushed the ultrasound cart out of the way and grabbed a scalpel out of a tray.

While that was happening, I swung the second camera over and pointed it at Dr. DuVal up at the horse's head. I was at the perfect angle to get the monitors right behind her as she continuously checked the horse and the machines, so I just left the camera running and turned back to the surgeons.

"We want to make our cut right beside the flexor tendon, so you just palpate that and get your spot. Feel it?"

Dr. Sanders reached up and felt the leg where he was pointing. "Do you push the tendon over or just go straight in beside it?"

"I usually clamp my thumb down right here, so it pops up a bit. That way you can hold the skin tight, and the tendon is easy to see. Then I just slice like this, one smooth cut through the skin about two inches long, nice and shallow. There are a few other structures in this area, so you want to open the skin, then spread it before you go deeper so you can see what you're cutting. Right there, that's a nerve, so we'll work around that, and the same with that vessel there. There's a ton of fascia right underneath here, so you'll feel a lot more resistance when you hit that. It's tougher than the skin. We'll spread again, and take a look, and right there, that's the tendon sheath. That's what we're looking for."

I zoomed in, trying to capture what he was pointing at with the scalpel handle. The camera screen was too small to see anything clearly, and I wished that I had a big monitor to plug the camera in to. If the shot was out of focus, or over-exposed, that was just too bad, because there were no retakes on a project like this. I was beginning to understand why movie sets needed so many people and so much equipment.

"I'm going to hold this open with the spreaders, and you cut through the tendon sheath," Dr. Hotchkiss was saying. "Just cut a little at a time. We don't want to damage the tendon or the nerves on the inside, we just want to get through the sheath. You've got this, it's just like the one we opened Monday. We're just doing something else once we get in there."

I adjusted the camera angle a bit so I could get her in the shot, and pulled the zoom back. It occurred to me that the other camera had been recording for a while, and the file was going to be massive if I didn't stop it. I reached over and hit the red button and spun back to catch the next bit.

"Right," Dr. Sanders said, taking the scalpel from him. "I've got it. Ready?"

He nodded, and she began cutting. I was surprised at how little blood there was in all of this. Erica had mentioned repeatedly in various podcasts that there was very little blood flow in the lower leg because there was no muscle at all below the hock. But knowing that and seeing it were two different things, and actually looking at the inside of a living horse's leg was giving me a whole new understanding of things.

Once they got through the tendon sheath, Dr. Hotchkiss took over again. "Okay, now we're in business. There's the nerve we're looking for. I'm just going to slide a clamp under it to isolate it so we don't cut anything else, and you can slice it right there."

Dr. Sanders didn't hesitate and made a clean cut across the nerve. I was impressed with her confidence. She had probably done dozens of surgeries at this point, but it still had to be nerve-wracking to have a senior surgeon standing right there, watching your every move. My hands would have been shaking too bad to hold the scalpel, much less cut the right thing. It was probably good that I was just running the camera.

With that done, Dr. Hotchkiss used a pair of scissors to cut into the fascia around the tendon. "See how there's no room in here? That lesion is causing the tendon to swell, but there's so much fascia and bone around it, it doesn't have any space to swell into. That's why it's so painful. We'll just give it some room here, and the PRP will help the lesion heal, and with the nerve cut, she should be able to stand on it, which is what we want. And that's it, time to close it up."

I glanced at the clock on the wall. Prep for surgery had taken nearly two hours, but the procedure itself was over in less than ten minutes. This was a lot different than Ernie's colic surgery, which had taken forever. It helped that it was nine in the morning, rather than midnight. Being well-rested and alert made it a lot better for me all the way around.

Dr. Hotchkiss sutured the incision closed and bandaged the whole lower leg. I moved the camera around in front of him to get a different angle, but realized halfway through the shot that my light and the other camera were visible in the background. Being a one-man camera crew in a surgery had proved to be far more complicated than shooting a video of Erica lecturing on things in our barn. I decided I needed an assistant in the future.

Things happened fast from that point. The anesthesia was turned off, the sheets removed, and the leg detached from the overhead crane. I hurried to get the cameras out of the way as they wheeled the table back out the door and over to a recovery room. I raced after them with a camera, but the horse was already in the air by the time I got the tripod set. I knew they were working against the clock to get him in the padded room and unhooked from everything before he started waking up, but it was impressive how fast they got that done. Less than two minutes after he rolled out of surgery, the recovery room door was closed, and suddenly it was a waiting game.

I pulled all my gear out of the operating room so they could clean it up for the next surgery. By the time I had it all packed up, the horse was standing, and the sounds of his muffled whinnies filled the hospital. It was probably a little scary to wake up in a small room with green padding covering every surface, not knowing how in the world you got there. Doubly so for a horse, as they need to be able to see another horse at all times, just so they know they aren't alone on an alien planet.

The hour drive home went by in a blur. My head was filled with thoughts and feelings and new perspectives, and I was simultaneously sure that it would take me days to mentally sort it out and terrified that I was going to forget half of it before that happened. Reality was probably somewhere in the middle.

Dr. Hotchkiss and his team were thrilled with the video once I got it all put together. They put it on their YouTube channel, and use it as a tool for helping horse owners get an idea of what the procedure is like if their horse needs one. I got to go back and shoot a laparoscopic ovariectomy, which was also a fascinating experience. The horse was standing for that procedure, sedated in the stocks while they went inside with a camera and tiny instruments and removed her ovary through a tiny slit in her abdomen.

So yeah, lots of exciting things have come along with being married to Erica. It has made my life so much fuller than it ever was before, and also filled my head up with a hodgepodge collection of weird horse knowledge. I'm great entertainment at a party, just don't ask me to brush your horse, or put a bridle on him. I still don't know much about that part of things!

16

The Great Aisleway Showdown

Horses are unique in their ability to take humans to our maximum emotional capacity in every direction. When you love your horse, you love him so much it makes your chest ache. When you're proud of your horse for his performance at a local show, it's the equivalent of getting ten gold medals at the Olympics. When your horse drives you crazy, you could axe murder him in front of a crowd of people. And when your horse gets hurt, it's the end of the world, even if he's injured himself a hundred times.

The other side of this coin is the emotional stability of the human in the relationship, or lack thereof. Horses will take us through our entire range, often on a daily basis, but if we don't have some sort of handle on ourselves, we're just along for the ride. That's a tough way to live.

Evelyn had been Erica's client since the day she bought the practice, way back in 2002. Her farm consisted of about twenty Arabs, plus or minus a few over the years. She didn't really do anything with them in terms of a sport or riding, she just liked having them. As a trust fund baby, she was able to provide everything they needed, and she did. Any horse that ended up at her house had hit the lottery.

The problem for Evelyn was that she didn't have great emotional management tools. She loved those horses so much that it became her whole life, her reason for living, and she couldn't stand to see one of them suffer in any way. And with twenty Arabs running around, she never went more than a few months without one of them having an injury, or a colic, or an eye ulcer, or a vague sense of unease that Evelyn couldn't tolerate because she wanted them to always be perfect. And by the time I came into the picture, Evelyn and her horses were all aging, and time just makes everything worse for both the mind and the body.

I'd been to Evelyn's farm a dozen times for emergencies, so I was accustomed to her anxiety. If it was a minor problem, she would call. If it was a serious problem, her husband, Richard, would call, as she would be sobbing and incapable of speaking coherently, although she would still be nearby to make sure that he passed on all the pertinent information and to confirm that we were on our way immediately.

One Saturday afternoon, Erica and I were holed up in the living room, soaking up the air conditioning and watching a European show jumping horse show on YouTube. It was August, and both the temperature and the humidity were uncomfortably high. We had just watched Beezie Madden make an amazing run in the jump off, and were discussing the amount of work it takes to compete at that level when the phone rang.

"Hello, Dr. Lacher."

"Hey Dr. Lacher, it's Richard. We've got a situation over here, and it looks like we need some help. Kawliga got himself in a jam."

There was a muffled exchange, and then Evelyn's hoarse voice came over the phone in a choked bellow. "He's bleeding out, Erica! He's not going to make it! Oh God, I can't even look at him, it's so bad! What are we going to do?"

"Sorry about that," Richard said, evidently having recovered the phone. "I don't think he's bleeding out, but he's cut up pretty good in a few places."

Erica finally managed to get a word in as we were putting on our shoes to leave. "What did he do?"

"Well, it's hot, so we put the big fan in the aisle, and opened up the doors so they could come stand in front of it if they wanted to. I don't know what started it, but I guess Kawliga and the fan got into it. He's covered in cuts and slices, and his back legs are stuck inside the fan blades."

"Oh, jeez," Erica said. "Unplug the fan, and hold him still the best you can. We'll be there in a minute."

I grabbed some tools, and by the time she hung up, we were already rolling down the driveway. Fortunately, Evelyn and Richard were only about ten minutes away. I parked in front of the barn, an old low building with open-sided stalls that had doors to both the center aisle and the outside paddock area. Erica pulled up some sedation in a syringe, and I grabbed a handful of towels and her headlamp. When we got inside, Evelyn was hugging Kawliga like she was never going to see him again while Richard attempted to hold him still.

"Oh, Erica, I'm so glad you're here," Evelyn cried, releasing Kawliga's neck as she turned. "This is just too much; I can't take it. We just got his eye healed up from the ulcer, and now we're probably going to lose him. And we just lost Peewee last year! What am I doing wrong?"

"It's just horses," Erica said. "Let me give him some drugs quick."

Like many older barns, the lighting wasn't very good, but the door was big and let in a lot of outside light. Kawliga was gray, and mostly on the white end of the gray spectrum, so the myriad slices, abrasions, and streaks of blood all over him were exceptionally prominent, even in the semi-gloom. His back legs were inside the housing of a mostly unrecognizable 48" fan that was lying on its side and smashed all to hell. Erica eased up beside him and slipped the needle in his neck, delivering the drugs that would keep him calm. Once that was done, she gave him a quick once over.

"Well, I don't think you're going to lose him," Erica said, walking slowly around the horse. "Most of this looks superficial. He's got a couple of deep slices, but they aren't near a joint, so that's good. Once the sedation kicks in, we'll get him out of the fan so we can see what the actual damage is."

"Oh, thank God!" Evelyn burst into tears all over again. "This is just too much. Why do they do this to me? I almost went to the house, there's so much blood everywhere."

"I don't know what set him off," Richard said. "We were down in the house, and all of the sudden it sounded like somebody was tearing the barn apart. When we got out here, it was already over, and he was standing just like this. I guess he ripped the plug out of the wall, so that was good. It wouldn't surprise me if he got shocked at some point during all that, but at least it didn't keep going. I didn't see any burn marks on him, but it's too dark to tell for sure."

I squatted down to look at the fan. Kawliga had bent the front grill around enough with repeated kicks that his hooves were able to get between the bars and go through the blades and belt to the back grill, which was also mangled. This wasn't going to be an easy extraction, and even with the sedation, it was going to be extremely dangerous. It didn't help that it was hot and stuffy in the barn. Was it ironic that the fan I needed in that moment was also the whole reason we were there in the first place?

"We're going to have to cut this thing apart," I said, standing up. "Once we get the grill cut away, I think we can bend the fan blades back enough to get his feet out. I just worry that he's going to try and get himself out once we start working on it. I don't want him to get hurt worse, or hurt us on accident."

"I'll give him more drugs if I need to," Erica said. "Do you have what you need to take it apart?"

I nodded. "Yeah, let me just grab some tools out of the truck."

A moment later, I was back. Erica took over managing the horse. I put the headlamp on, and used a small set of bolt cutters to cut the bars of the grill away, one at a time. Richard bent them back as I cut, and we worked our way around the left foot. A deep cut between the fetlock and the hock was still pumping out blood, which was congealing in the dirt below and making it hard to see past the fan blade. Once that side was done, Richard took the cutters and began on his side, and I bent the bars back. When the last piece of grill was cut away from the feet, we cut it into sections and removed the whole thing. After ten minutes, I was pouring out sweat. I dropped the bolt cutters and grabbed a towel.

"Okay, Erica," I said, mopping my forehead. "I think we're ready to bend the fan blades out of the way, but that's going to put my face right beside his foot. Is he still knocked out?"

Kawliga's head was drooping down to his knees, which was a good sign. Erica tapped his eyelid, and he barely twitched. "I think he's as good as he's going to get. Just keep yourself as far back as you can, and if his leg starts to move, get out of there."

I grabbed the bloody fan blade with the towel and glanced at Richard. "I need you to hold that side still so it doesn't hit his other leg and set him off. Once I get this one bent up, I'll hold it, and you bend that one."

"Got it." Richard took a towel off the stack and gripped the blade in front of him. There was no way for either of us to keep our heads as far back as I would have liked, but sometimes that's the situation. I got into position on my side and tried to fold the blade up vertical. It didn't move.

"Huh," I grunted, trying again to no avail. "This thing must be made out of titanium or something."

I grabbed the oversized pair of channel lock pliers and adjusted the jaws down flat. With the sixteen-inch handles, I had significantly more leverage, and the blade slowly bent upright, folding in half at a crease from the earlier damage. They also gave me a bit more distance from Kawliga's feet, which I appreciated. I probably should have started out with the pliers, but in the heat of the moment, it didn't occur to me until I needed them.

I handed the pliers to Richard, and he slowly bent the other two blades out of the way. It took some effort on his part, as the one blade without any damage was much harder to bend. I held it still as best I could while he worked it from different angles, and at last, it gave in.

We stopped to rest, and assess the situation. I couldn't tell if there was anything holding him now, with all the bloody mud covering the bottom grill. I used a towel to wipe the grime away around his left foot. The toe was sticking down between two bent bars on the grill, but I was pretty sure he could just lift his foot out of that.

"How does it look on your side?" I asked, handing Richard another towel.

He shoved a pile of congealed blood out of the way, and I shined the light around the foot. "I think it's okay," he said at last. "He's still running blood on this one, so it's hard to see, but it looks like he's clear, as long as he picks his feet up when he steps out of it."

"Oh God, I know he's bleeding out," Evelyn muttered from the shadows. "He's been bleeding too long."

I stood up and stretched my back, ignoring Evelyn for the moment. "Okay, I guess we're ready to move. Once he takes a step, he has to keep going, though. We've basically turned this thing into a blender, so don't let him step back into it." I regretted the words as soon as they came out of my mouth, but the damage was done.

"Oh no, don't say that!" Evelyn cried. "I can't deal with any more today. Is he going to be okay? I can't even look. Erica, tell me he's okay."

Erica took over, rescuing me. "I've got him. Let's get everyone out of the way. The drugs are going to be wearing off in a minute. As soon as he starts waking up, I'll walk him forward out of the fan. Justin, when he starts to move, you wave your arms and make him want to go. Got it?"

I nodded and wiped my face again. My shirt was soaked by this time, and even my shorts were starting to drip sweat from the hem. While we waited for Kawliga to wake up, I gathered all the pieces of grill and carried them outside, along with my tools. I rinsed everything off at the hose, including myself, and took a good long drink. When I got back inside, it was time to move.

"Okay, here we go," Erica said. "Come on boy, let's go." Erica raised his head up, and Richard and I began waving our arms and shouting. At first, he didn't budge, but when I clapped my hands, he jerked forward and stepped out of the remains of the fan. Erica kept the momentum going and half-drug him right out the front door to the water hose. I sagged in relief as they walked away.

"Oh, thank you, Jesus," Evelyn shouted, bursting in to tears yet again. "Don't take my baby yet, I'm not ready!"

We followed them out the doorway and into the light. I squinted as my pupils adjusted, grateful that we were under a tree and not in direct sunshine. The next step was hosing him off. Most of the blood was dried by this time, so it took a bit to get him cleaned up. Erica soaked him down to cool him off, and once he was gray again, we were finally able to get a full assessment of the damage.

"What do you think about the one that's still bleeding?" I asked quietly.

"I think we're going to bandage it and let it clot and fix itself," she said. "The other option is to lay him down, put a tourniquet above it, and try to ligate it. It's not an artery, so

I don't think there's any advantage to doing that. A vein will heal up on its own pretty well."

I nodded. "That's probably the safer option, right? He's got to be over twenty."

"Well, not knocking them out is always the safer option, it doesn't matter how old they are. But yeah, for a variety of reasons, I don't want to do that."

I stepped back as she finished her exam. Richard and Evelyn stood at his head, awaiting the report.

"For all of this, it looks like I'm only going to need to suture two spots," Erica said. "He opened a vessel there, but it's not too serious, so I think once we get that stitched up and close this flap over here, he'll be all set. We'll keep a bandage on those for a few days, but everything else will be fine. It's mostly scrapes and nicks."

"You're a lucky son of a gun," Richard said. "I don't know how you managed to pull that off without cutting your leg off."

"Don't say that," Evelyn said. "Oh, don't say that! We need to go through the barn and pull out everything that he might be able to kick through. What if he does it again?"

"It's an old, wooden barn," Richard said. "He can probably kick through any of the walls if he tried. You can't protect him from everything."

They argued on as Erica sutured the two main lacerations. I held his halter, but Kawliga wasn't trying to go anywhere. The sedation might have been wearing off, but he had been through a pretty draining experience, and I knew he had to be sore. He probably wouldn't be moving a whole lot for several days, despite Evelyn's fears for the worst.

"Okay, who wants a class on bandaging legs?" Erica

asked. "You're going to do this every other day for at least a week."

"Richard, you know I can't hardly stand it," Evelyn said. "I just hate to see them in pain. You'll change his bandages, won't you?" She looked at him imploringly, as if they hadn't had this exact same conversation a hundred times before. I suppressed a laugh, but just barely.

"I always do," Richard said. "I could do with a refresher, though. I haven't had to do it in a while."

Erica and Richard bandaged the leg together, and Evelyn walked over to the fence to gaze at the other horses until they were done. I wondered how she got through life like this, loving her horses but being unable to manage the challenges that inevitably come with them. Horses are the physical embodiment of the yin and yang. To have the good, you also get the bad. Fortunately for these horses, Richard was here to keep the balance. In a way, Richard and Evelyn were their own yin yang, as were Erica and myself.

Once the bandages were applied, I helped Richard clear the rest of the fan out of the barn. Out in the daylight, I was finally able to get a decent look at it, and it was a sight to behold. Between Kawliga's efforts, and then Richard and I having our go at it, it looked like it had been shot by a tank. Maybe twice. It was hard to imagine what sparked the incident, but if there was ever a question about who would win between a horse and a shop fan, I now knew that the answer was no one. Kawliga didn't look much better than the fan, and he could have come out of it even worse.

Life is unpredictable at the best of times. Life with horses? As people have shown me over and over again, it's a team sport. The horses have a playbook with thousands of ideas in it, and the best we can do is hope to have what we need to get them through whichever thing they do at any given moment. As Richard pointed out, we can't protect them from everything. Besides, if horses didn't need to be rescued once in a while, how could they be sure that we love them?

17

Halloween Horse Shows

Erica and I enjoy Christmas, mostly because it's a chance for us to spend some time with our chosen family in Atlanta. Outside of that aspect, holidays really aren't a big deal for us. We don't give each other presents for any occasion, a deal we struck at the beginning of our relationship that has stood the test of time as a great decision. We're not 'stuff' people, so we agreed to spend our money and time on trips and experiences rather than gifts.

The exception to the minimal holiday excitement tendency is Halloween. As you might recall, Erica and I were married at the end of October back in 2015, and we had a costume wedding. There's just something liberating about dressing up and letting our inner child have fun. For me, part of that is probably based on a childhood where I was never allowed to participate in that kind of stuff. For Erica, it's more that she gets to not be Dr. Lacher, business owner, veterinarian, extremely responsible person, at least for a few hours.

Instead of going to costume parties to have our fun, we go to a local horse show. If you've never been to a Halloween horse show with a costume class, you've got to find one near you and experience that! I don't know if you can have more fun than being immersed in the creative joy of themed costumes for horse and human. And I'm not talking about professional costumes, mass-produced and available at a dealer near you. I'm talking about a labor of love, sweated over in the tack room for a month, held together with craft paint, glue, tape, and determination (and maybe some hay string).

One of the many reasons that Cai is the perfect horse for Erica is that she isn't bothered by a cape, and Erica loves a cape flapping in the wind as she canters around a jumper course. One of the things that drew her to Cai in the beginning was a picture of Cai and a little girl dressed up in a costume. Ernie, her OTTB (off-the-track thoroughbred) show horse for ten years, was not cool with that kind of thing at all. He was a spook first, ask questions later kind of guy. So, Erica had to wait a long time to do this, and she was ready.

"We need to get our costume idea put together," she said one afternoon.

"Costume for what?" I asked, suddenly sure that I had forgotten something important.

"That Halloween horse show," she said, as if it were the most obvious thing in the world. "Cai and I need a costume."

I glanced at my computer. "It's April 4th."

She nodded vigorously. "I know, we're already behind. That's why we need to get going on it."

Over the years, I had finally started to learn that there are times to say when I think something is ridiculous, and there are times to just go along with it. I decided on the spot that this was a good time to go along with it, but I still had to put a bit of snark on it. "Yeah, of course. I didn't want to pressure you about it, but we've barely got six months left to get this done."

She stuck her tongue out at me. "I'm serious. We'll need six months to plot this out, make it, do some trial runs to make sure Cai can jump a course with it, make corrections, and all that. It's not like we have a bunch of free time to commit to it."

That was the logic I needed to hear. In our lives, free time was counted in minutes here and there. She was right: between work, being on-call, recording videos and podcasts, riding horses, writing books and blogs, and trying to keep the farm functioning, it probably would take six months to get a costume put together.

"Okay, what kind of ideas do you have?" I asked. "Are you trying to make a costume for Cai, too?"

"Of course, you can't just have a rider in costume and nothing on the horse, that wouldn't be any fun. I want to wear a cape. That's what I've got so far."

Now that we were doing something creative with a critical thinking component, I was getting into the spirit. "A cape. Okay, that puts us in the superhero realm, or possibly a vampire. Are you leaning towards an existing character, or do you want to do something original?"

"Probably existing. What female superheroes wear capes?"

"Supergirl, Wonder Woman, Batgirl… it's too bad Cat Woman doesn't have a cape, since you're a borderline crazy cat lady."

"Ooh, Wonder Woman could work. Cai can be the invisible plane!"

That conversation turned into our first serious Halloween project since our wedding. We used an off-the-rack costume for Erica, and put most of our effort into designing and building Cai's outfit. Turning a horse into an invisible airplane was no easy task.

Erica's costume had come with a crown and a necklace, and that was our first challenge to figure out. We ended up gluing the crown to her helmet, which actually worked out really well, but there didn't seem to be a good way of putting the necklace on that didn't end up jabbing her in the throat going over a jump.

"I think I have an idea," I said. We were out back in the riding arena, trying out different configurations while getting Cai used to the flapping cape. "What if we glued the necklace on to the browband on the bridle? Then Cai has some sparkly bits and a splash of color on her head, and it would match the crown on your helmet."

"It's way too wide," Erica said, pulling it off her neck and looking at it doubtfully. "We'd have to cut it down."

I shrugged. "I don't think that would take anything away from it. We'd still have a half-inch gold band across her head with a big red stone in the middle. With her forelock hanging over it, I think it would be perfect."

With that decided, we moved on to the rest of Cai's costume. We got a dark blue sleazy, which is a terrible name for a piece of spandex that covers the horse's neck and shoulders, and hand-painted a field of white stars on it. It took three coats of paint, but it finally came together. Last were the red streamers which we glued to Cai's jumping boots, so they looked like little glittery capes when she was running.

The whole costume came together way better than I imagined. When we finally got to the horse show in October, I think I was more excited than Erica. My heart swelled up with pride as she rode up to the schooling ring to warm up with her trainer. Cai was a dark chocolate bay, and with her winter coat starting to come in, she was even darker. The gold headband and white stars on the sleazy really popped, and with Erica's shiny blue skirt over her breeches and red cape streaming out behind her, you couldn't help but stare as she rode past.

There were at least a dozen other kids and adults in costume at the show. Several had gone with the traditional knight in armor, with a mile of aluminum foil wrapped around both horse and rider. One of my favorites was a horse that was covered in handprints, each a different color. The rider was covered in horseshoe prints. Very clever!

Erica and Cai had a rail in the jump off and ended up in third place, but they won the costume contest, which was way more important. We celebrated with an ice cream cone, and some soaked alfalfa cubes for Cai. On the ride home, my head was already spinning with ideas for the next year's costume.

"I want in on the action next time," I said. "I think

it would be hilarious if we could come up with a themed costume for all three of us."

"Yeah! I agree. Any ideas?"

"Not yet, but I'm working on it."

Over the next few months, we considered tons of ideas, and rejected most of them for various reasons.

"What if we did this same costume again next year?" I asked. "Then we just have to get me a Superman outfit."

Erica shook her head before I could even finish the question. "I can't wear the same costume twice in a row, no way. Also, Cai sweat-stained the sleazy so bad we'd have to make another one, and I don't think either of us wants to paint stars again."

"That's fair," I said. "The stars were definitely a time-consuming thing."

"Also, if you're wanting to make a video for YouTube, then it needs to be something we haven't done before. We already posted a bunch of pictures of the Wonder Woman show."

"Okay, you've sold me on that," I said. "Also, you're the hero. I want to find something where the male figure isn't necessarily the leader."

"Well, that certainly narrows the choices," Erica said. "I don't think you're going to find that in the superhero world. But I still want a cape."

I thought for a moment. "Doesn't the Queen of Hearts have a cape? I could be the jack, and we could make Cai into a heart horse."

"Hhmmm." Erica pulled out her phone and did a quick search. "It's not really a cape, but it could become one. We can put it on the 'maybe' list."

A few weeks later, we were driving, and a song by Eminem came on the radio. It was one of my favorites of his, and as we listened, the music video came to mind. Suddenly, it hit me: this was what we had been looking for!

"I got it," I shouted as I slammed on the brakes and turned into the first available parking lot. "This is our costume!"

"What are you talking about?" Erica looked up from her phone in a near-panic. "Did we hit something?"

"No, the song!" I grabbed my phone and pulled up the music video on YouTube for her. "Eminem is wearing a Robin costume in this video, as in Batman and Robin, which has a cape. Dr. Dre is wearing a black leather jacket and sunglasses, and they're riding around in a yellow Ferrari. You can be Eminem, the hero. Cai can be the Ferrari, and I'll be Dr. Dre. It's perfect!"

She gave me a doubtful look. "Are they just driving around?"

I forced myself to slow down and be coherent. "The premise of the video is that there is a rap emergency, which is that there aren't any good rappers. Dr. Dre reports the emergency to Eminem, and as the hero, he jumps in the rap-mobile with Dr. Dre and they race off to save the world from the crisis. Kind of like we do with horse emergencies."

A smile crept across her face. "Okay, I'll admit that I love the idea, but do you think anyone will get it? How recognizable is a twenty-year-old music video costume?"

"Who cares?" I said. "We'll know. And we can shoot a video spoof of this video, and make it horse-doctor themed. Our own music video! Come on, how fun would that be?"

To be fair, I'm a much bigger Hip Hop fan than Erica,

so I probably loved this idea more than she did. But she went along with it, and we began to plot it out. Like the Wonder Woman idea from the year before, the people part of the costume was much easier than the horse part. I already had everything I needed to be Dr. Dre, which was my motorcycle jacket and a pair of sunglasses. One down, two to go.

We found a good quality Robin costume with a nice cape for Erica, which was the most important thing, as you know by now. It was glossy black on the outside with a yellow interior and rippled nicely in the sunshine. The rest of the costume was a questionable shade of lime green and orange, but her tall black riding boots and black helmet complimented it nicely. The only real work we had to do was make a backwards E to go over the R on the chest. Eminem had the backwards E in his video, and since that worked with Erica too, we went with it.

"How do we turn Cai into a yellow Ferrari?" I asked. "Can we paint her?"

"We probably could, but it would be a lot easier to get a full-body slinky. They come in every color of the rainbow." She pulled one up on the computer so I could see a picture of it. The image showed a horse covered in spandex from nose to tail, with holes for the eyes and ears. It was skintight, bright yellow, and perfect in every way.

"That's exactly what we need! We can make some big Ferrari symbols to go on it, and I think it'll look amazing. If nothing else, the giant yellow horse will definitely draw attention!"

"I just have to make sure she can jump in it," Erica said. "The leg straps might be a problem."

"We can always cut them off and glue some Velcro on

there and put them wherever they fit best. With the saddle and girth on her, you might not need straps at all."

It took a week for the slinky to arrive. While we waited, I asked Cassie, one of our more artistic technicians, for some tips on making the badging.

"I need two big Ferrari emblems," I said. "One on each flank. The slinky is mostly spandex, which we learned last year is really hard to paint on. How would you go about it?"

Cassie thought for a moment. "I think I'd get a piece of yellow fabric and paint the black horses on that. You can get some thin ribbon for the red, white and green striping across the top. Then it's just a matter of gluing them on the slinky."

I nodded, impressed with her problem-solving skills. "I like it. Now I just have to figure out how to paint the horse. That's a little beyond my skills."

"I'd be happy to make them for you," she said. "I love this whole costume idea, and it would be fun to do."

By the middle of September, we had the whole thing put together, and it was fantastic! I couldn't believe how good Erica and Cai looked. We did end up cutting the leg straps off so they wouldn't rub, but we didn't need them anyway. Erica decided to do a full-dress rehearsal on a Saturday in early October, just to make sure we had all the bases covered, and it's a good thing we did.

I was filming with my phone so Erica could see what it all looked like. They went over the first jump, then another, and everything looked fine to me. After the third jump, I noticed that she was turning a bit weird, and after the fourth jump, she pulled up. I turned off the camera and jogged over.

"What's up?" I asked.

"It's this mask," she said. "I can't see anything that's not right in front of me. There's no peripheral vision at all."

"Huh," I said. "The Lone Ranger made it look easy."

She hopped down, handed me her helmet and the reins, and removed the mask. "I think we can widen the eyeholes and make it work. I might take a bit off the top too, so my helmet doesn't hit it every time I land. That's killing the bridge of my nose."

She did some surgery on the mask, and after a few tweaks, it was functional. When she was satisfied, we moved on to the next task.

"Okay, while you're both in full costume, let's go ahead and do some filming for the music video," I said. "I think it makes sense to shoot the one that involves Cai first, then we can get her back in her stall, and she'll be done."

"Do you want to leave the saddle on?"

I thought for a second. "No, I think it looks better without it if you're not on her. Hopefully she didn't sweat too badly."

Erica got Cai unsaddled while I got the camera equipment set up. The scene was going to be Erica and Cai running out of the barn, side by side, in costume, responding to the emergency. After countless hundreds of hours of groundwork, Erica was excited to show off Cai's skills. The plan was for Cai to run beside her, no halter, no nothing. It was probably a small detail that would go unnoticed by most, but other people who had done liberty work with their own horses would recognize it for what it was.

"Okay, I'm going to do it with the halter on a few times first," Erica said. "Just to remind her what we're doing here."

I nodded. "Good plan. She hasn't done it in a week. And that will give me a chance to practice the pan on the camera and make sure I've got everything set right."

They started out in the barn aisle and picked up a trot. I was out front and off to one side, and as they came by, I swung the camera around to track them. I had to adjust the light settings, as they were coming out of a dark barn and into full daylight. By the third time, we both felt like we were ready to remove the halter and do it for real.

"Okay, I'm going to record this, even though it's a practice run," I said. "Just in case it's perfect."

Erica nodded. "Okay, here we go."

She clucked, and they came out at a trot. As soon as they cleared the mounting block, Cai veered off to the right and took off. Erica gave chase, and I knew within seconds that the blooper reel was going to be better than the actual video. Erica in a Robin costume, chasing Cai in a bright yellow banana suit around the farm? Now *that's* good entertainment!

It took nearly five minutes to catch Cai. She ran one way, then another, doubling back if Erica got too close. After the first few passes, I started to feel guilty about standing there filming, so I turned the camera off and went to help. We managed to steer her back into the barn at last, and she walked into her stall and started eating hay like nothing had happened.

"Maybe she's just showing off for the camera," I said.

Erica was huffing and puffing beside me. "She did great for the first three strides."

I laughed. "In terms of horses being horses, she was technically perfect. She pacified you by doing it right for months, lulled you into a false sense of security, and then left you hanging when the stakes were highest. It was a flawless execution."

"Yeah, the other horses probably loved it." She wiped the sweat off her forehead. "Okay, let's try it again."

"Same thing?" I asked. "At liberty?"

She thought for a moment. "Maybe I'll just keep a hand on her. I can hold on to the Velcro bit that goes under her jaw."

We got back in position and tried again. This time they were perfect, and trotted out like they had a dozen times in practice, except for Erica's hand on Cai's chin. They circled back, and we reviewed the footage.

"What do you think?" I asked. "It looks pretty good like that, but we can go for no hands if you want to do it again."

Erica looked at her watch, then looked at Cai. "I've already got five thousand steps in today chasing her around. I really don't want to do that again. But on the other hand, we practiced this a lot. I hate to give up without a clean run when I know we can do it."

"It's a tough position," I agreed. "I'll do whatever you want to do."

"Let's do it one more time. If it doesn't work, we'll go with what we've got."

I clapped my hands and used my best movie director voice. "Okay! Here we go. Places, everyone! Camera rolling in five."

The third run never even made it in frame on the video. As soon as Erica started to jog out of the aisle, Cai stopped, turned around, and went back to her stall.

Erica threw up her hands in defeat. "I guess we'll go with take two. This just isn't happening today."

I tried to console her. "Everything goes better in practice when there's no one there to see it. All of the best performances my band ever had were in the living room. Don't sweat it, it's going to be fine."

"Well, what do you want to shoot next?" she asked, shaking it off like a pro.

I consulted the shot list. "We can do the two barn aisle scenes now. The rest of it happens in the truck, and that has to be at night."

It took me a few tries to get the lights set in the right places, and then we started practicing our lines. There had been minimal planning on the specifics of these scenes, and Erica and I were winging it. It's how we do most things, to be honest.

"I'm going to just mimic the Eminem video," I said. "Dr. Dre starts it off by saying *Marshall, it sounds like an S.O.S.* I'll just say Dr. Lacher instead of Marshall."

"Who's Marshall?"

"That's Eminem's name. Anyway, Eminem says *Holy wack unlyrical lyrics, Andre. You're **** right!*" And then Dr. Dre says, *To the rap-mobile.* So we just have to figure out something to put in place of *unlyrical lyrics.* And probably no swearing."

"Yeah, let's keep it G rated. Something like *Holy Unruly Horses, Justin.* Something about them being disagreeable, or getting themselves in trouble."

I pulled up the thesaurus on my phone. "Disorderly, impetuous, intemperate, obstreperous, opinionated, rebellious, wayward."

"Ooh, obstreperous. That's a good one."

It *was* a good word, but it turned out that trying to remember it, much less spit it out fast and smooth when you just learned it, was really hard. Once we added in choreography, it got worse. Being a cast and crew of two is hard.

After an hour of effort, we felt like we had some usable footage. It wasn't perfect, but it didn't need to be. This was supposed to be a fun video, after all. The second scene seemed simple, as it was just a shot of us sitting in the barn aisle, bobbing our heads in time to the music. I set the cameras and lights, brought up the song on my phone, and hit record.

As a former musician, I feel like I have a decent sense of rhythm, at least enough to nod my head with a song. And maybe I did when I was younger, and I lost it somewhere along the way. I don't know. But my timing wasn't quite on. And by the third take, I realized that Erica has no sense of rhythm at all. Zero. Zilch.

After about ten minutes of starting the song over and trying to get us in sync, I gave up in exasperation. "This is just going to be a spoof about our whiteness and complete lack of rhythm," I said. "If we can't get it right here, we're not going to get the vehicle shots coordinated either, because that's all that happens in them."

"I think people will get the humor in that," Erica said. "We look ridiculous, right? What more could you ask for in a spoof video?"

As usual, she was right. "I'm probably taking this too serious."

"You are," she said. "Try to remember the purpose of this. It's not the actual rap video."

That helped me get my perspective straightened out, and I was able to get back to having fun with it. It was good that she pointed it out to me, because once we got to the vehicle shots that night, we were really all over the place. Instead of trying to make it perfect, I just let the cameras roll and had a good time with it.

Watching Erica have an absolute blast doing her rap dancing in the passenger seat turned out to be one of the highlights of my life. She had such a look of pure joy on her face that I couldn't help but get caught up in the moment. Here we were, sitting in the cab of the truck at eight o'clock at night in our driveway, dressed up in costumes and making memories that I hope I'll never lose. No matter how the video came out in the end, I was thankful to have that experience captured for posterity. And I have a bunch of footage of me just grinning like an idiot as I watched her live fully and completely in the moment.

The last piece of the video was the horse show. I was both excited and nervous about our costumes. I was already used to being one of the only horse show husbands in attendance but being a forty-six-year-old guy dressed up in a costume that no one was going to understand without context suddenly seemed like a questionable idea. It was fine at home, even on camera, but going out in public brought on a whole different level of anxiety. At least I could hide behind the camera for part of it.

There was a surprising lack of costumed horses at the show. There were a few, to include a princess on a unicorn that was pretty good, but nothing like the year before. I was really disappointed. Erica and Cai looked fantastic, but with everyone else riding in their class in breeches and jackets, it took a lot of the fun out of it. She won the costume class, of course, with only a handful of people in the running, although she had a few rails on the course and wound up seventh in the standings. But we suited up and showed up, and I got a great video of her and Cai jumping fences in costume, cape flapping and the whole nine yards. It was a good day!

The video is on the Springhill Equine Veterinary Clinic YouTube channel, if you want to have a good laugh. Just go to YouTube and type *Springhill Equine Veterinary* into the search bar. That will bring up our channel, and you can scroll down our video list and find it. You'll know it when you see it. And you can check out the Horse Girl videos while you're there, and anything else that catches your eye!

Being married to Erica has taught me a lot of things. When I try to make a list, it all ends up being business stuff, like how to run a good business, and the importance of having a great culture in the clinic, and how to work seven days a week without catching your brain on fire. But she's also taught me how important it is to make time for fun, and to have fun with the things I'm doing. It's so easy for me to get wrapped up in perfectionism, and trying to get approval from my dad, who's been dead since 2004, and a lot of other things that don't actually mean anything in reality.

Sometimes I have to remind Erica not to take things so seriously, like when she was trying to trot Cai out of the barn, but usually it's the other way around. Erica finds joy in the moment with what she's doing, and shows me that those moments *are* life, that there is no 'later' that I'm working toward, no point in the future where I'll stop and enjoy myself, and no accolade from someone else that will make me feel better about who I am or what I do. Time well spent is about living in the moment, and being happy with who I am, and who I'm with. It doesn't even matter what the activity is, it's about our relationship with ourselves and those we love. So go make your rap video, whatever that is for you, and don't worry about making it perfect. It will be anyway.

18

Flying Solo

I met Erica in 2014, and since then, I've done an awful lot of things I never expected to do. For example, I didn't think I was capable of writing a book, and now I've written eight. I never thought I'd go snorkeling around the Great Blue Hole in Belize or stand on top of a Mayan ruin in the middle of the rainforest in Guatemala, but now I've done both.

Prior to 2014, I didn't know what a horse show was. I knew about rodeos, and horse racing, and that was about it. I'd never heard of dressage, or show jumping, or driving, or halter classes, or western pleasure, or any of the plethora of equine sport disciplines that exist. So, when I went to my first hunter jumper show with Erica, it was a whole new world to me.

I really like spending time with Erica, so I always go with her when she shows her horse. The number of horse show husbands is really low, at least at the shows we go to, so I know I'm unusual in my participation. But I like driving the truck and trailer, and I like videoing things, so it's a win all the way around for me. Even with my high level of involvement in that, I never expected to go to a horse show without Erica, but it happened. I didn't ride her horse, just to be clear. I hauled it to the show, where her trainer rode the horse, and then I brought it home. But still, I count that as something I never expected to do.

And at the very top of things that I've done with Erica that I would never dream of doing alone is responding to a horse emergency. I consider myself a great horse ambulance driver, and a mediocre emergency technician, and that's about it. I might be married to one of the most amazing equine veterinarians in the world, but I'm very clear about my role. I drive the truck and carry the stuff, and she manages the situations. Usually.

In the spring of 2023, Erica's aunt lost a long, painful battle with cancer. Due to scheduling conflicts, the celebration of life didn't happen until midsummer, but if you have to go from Florida to Washington State, July is a pretty good time to do it. Erica and her mother flew to Seattle on a Thursday, with a return trip planned for the following Monday, and I stayed home to manage the farm and the vet clinic.

There was a lot going on at the clinic that demanded my time on Friday, and I was really looking forward to a quiet weekend of feeding critters, writing, and editing. After a flurry of phone calls, making decisions, answering emails, and helping out with a few horses, I finally made it home and went to bed exhausted.

Saturday morning, I woke up about 5:30, feeling refreshed and ready to go. I did a light workout, fed the horses and brought them in, fed the dogs and cats, ate breakfast, took a shower, and settled down in front of the computer for a blissfully uninterrupted writing marathon. No one was home to pull me away or interrupt my train of thought, which was rare, and I intended to take advantage of every second of it. That lasted about ten minutes.

I had my phone on the desk just in case Erica called me, or Dr. Hanks, who was on call. As a business owner, you can never go completely off the radar. I had just finished reading what I had written in my last session and got caught up on where I left off when the phone buzzed with a new text message.

Are you home?

It was from Kim, a client and friend who had a training barn just down the road from us. If she had texted me this early, something was wrong.

Yes, I'm here, but Erica's out of town. What's up?

Dale's got his shoe stuck in the fence, and I'm up in Georgia at my dad's. The girls are at the barn. Can you help them get him out? He's not hurt, just stuck.

My dreams of a quiet morning of writing evaporated, but were immediately replaced with a sense of excitement. This was an emergency, but it was one I could handle. Nine years of training, and it was finally my time to shine!

Headed that way now.

I ran down the stairs two at a time, and grabbed some tools out of the feed room on my way to the truck. Three minutes later I was pulling up at Kim's place. Emerson, Cathy, and Ophie were surrounding a horse in a paddock near the barn, and I headed in their direction. All three were sixteen-year-old horse girls, and I had known them for years from hanging out at Kim's.

"What's up, gang?" I called, making my way around the corner of the barn to where they stood.

"Justin's here!" A chorus of cheers greeted me. It was funny to see them here in charge of the farm. They seemed like little kids, but probably only because I had known them when they were ten. When I was sixteen, I was very capable and responsible, and realizing I wasn't extending the same expectation to these girls made me feel old and judgey. I reminded myself that they had discovered the problem and handled it perfectly, and I should give them credit for that.

I slowly walked up to them on the outside of the fence, trying not to spook Dale. He was an eighteen-year-old Oldenburg, and as a lesson horse, he was probably bombproof, but I didn't want to risk him trying to back away from me and hurting himself. "Dale, what did you do?"

"He paws when he eats," Emerson said, pointing to the gouges in the dirt. "I think he just dug it out around the fence enough to hook his shoe on the bottom wire."

"The farrier was here on Thursday," Cathy added. "I think Dale is just trying to make him have to come back and fix his shoe."

"That sounds like a horse," I agreed, dropping down on one knee. The bottom of the no-climb fence had been buried in the dirt at one point, but between the horses walking the inside of the fence and creating a packed trail several inches deep and the rain washing the edges of the path out, the wire had become exposed and was curled into the pasture a few inches. There were several places in our own pastures at home that looked exactly the same and getting those fixed suddenly jumped up on my priority list.

Dale was standing calmly, and Cathy was holding his halter and feeding him treats to keep him distracted. The bottom wire on the fence was near the middle of his foot, between the shoe and the hoof. I was guessing that it was up against the nails holding the shoe on. None of the wires were broken, or even bent very much, so he hadn't struggled once he got caught, which was amazing. In this same situation, a lot of horses would panic, pull the fence down, rip their shoe off and probably half their hoof wall, get tangled in the wire and lacerate themselves all over, and then run down the road, dragging a mile of fence along with them.

"Okay, let's make a plan," I said. "Ophie, you hold his foot still, while Emerson cuts his leg off at the knee. Cathy, you manage his head, and I'll stand over here and video it all so you can put it on Snap Chat later. Is everybody ready?"

Dale knickered and bobbed his head, and the girls burst out laughing.

"I don't think Dale likes that plan," Emerson said. "What other ideas do you have?"

I shrugged. "Well, I guess I could just cut the wire and pull it out of his shoe, but it doesn't seem near as dramatic."

"I think that's a way better plan," Cathy said. "Let's go with that one."

"Yeah," Ophie agreed. "We can just tell everyone it was dramatic."

"Okay, I guess we'll do that." I pushed some of the loose dirt away from the fence. "I'm going to cut from this side, just to keep me safe since my head is down here by his foot. Let's try to keep him still, but if he decides to leave, let him go. I don't want anybody getting hurt."

I decided to cut the wire right up against the vertical strand on both sides so there wouldn't be any sharp pieces for him to lacerate himself on once he was loose. It was going to leave a bit of a hole in the fence, but I felt like that was the safest approach. There were two vertical strands to cut, and then the bottom wire on each side of the foot, for a total of four cuts. I had to be fast, as he was likely to try and leave once he realized he could move the foot.

"He's going to have the wire in his shoe still, so when I get these cut, don't let him go anywhere other than taking a step back. I'll come around there and figure out the next part." I pushed a little more dirt away so I had a clean approach to all four spots I needed to cut. "Ready?"

They nodded. "Ready."

I started on the inside bottom, and quickly worked my way around to the outside. It only took a few seconds to make the cuts, and Dale didn't even twitch. I stood up and jogged over to the gate and came back up the other side of the fence.

"Dale, you did a good job, buddy," I said, patting him on the neck. "Now let's see if we can get the wire out without taking your shoe off."

"Do you want me to hold his foot up?" Emerson asked.

"Sure, that would be great."

She squeezed the chestnut on his leg, and he obediently lifted his foot. I marveled at how nice it was to work on a horse that was used to being handled and didn't mind being compliant. It almost seemed too easy.

His shoe and frog were packed with dirt, and I carefully cleaned it out as much as I could to see what the situation was. The shoe was still tight on the foot, and I couldn't see any damage to the hoof wall or the sole.

"Alright, I'm going to cut the wire right up against the inside of the shoe, and then we'll pull it out the other side. Do you have him?"

Emerson nodded. "Got him."

I clipped the wire and handed the loose piece to Ophie. "Here, don't lose this, or he'll end up sticking it in his eye somehow."

She giggled and closed her fist around it.

Pulling the remaining wire out from under his shoe was much harder than the rest had been. Emerson braced his foot against her knee, and I pried it through a bit at a time. It took nearly thirty seconds, but at last, it was out. I handed that piece to Ophie as well, and stood up slowly, stretching my back.

"Let's walk him around a few steps and see if he's lame," I said. "If he's moving okay, we'll go up to the barn and wash his foot off and double check everything."

Cathy backed Dale away from the fence and led him in a slow circle. I bent down and folded the fence back so there weren't any corners poking out and grabbed my tools.

"I think he looks fine," Emerson said. "You want us to take him to the barn?"

"Yeah, he looks pretty good," I said. "Of course, I can't tell if a horse is limping until it's three-legged lame. That's why I take Dr. Lacher on emergencies, she's the lameness expert."

"She's the everything expert," Cathy said. "She's like a horse knowledge ninja."

We slowly walked to the barn. I did my best to see if one of Dale's hips or shoulders dropped more than the other, or if his head was bobbing more than it should, as Erica had shown me a hundred times, but if he was off, I couldn't see it. Subtle lameness was never going to be my thing.

We stopped at the water hose, and I grabbed a hoof pick out of the basket and got his foot good and clean. Once the mud was gone, his frog was bright white, since the farrier had just trimmed him. That made it easy to see everything, and the only thing I could see out of the ordinary was a slight depression where the wire had been. The nails were still tight, and the shoe wasn't bent or sprung. It seemed unlikely that Dale could have gotten himself that stuck and then walked away unscathed, but I couldn't find anything wrong with his foot.

"He looks pretty perfect," I said. "Let's walk him up and down the aisle so we can see him move on the concrete. Who's the lameness expert here? Cathy? Ophie?"

"Not me," Ophie said. "I can feel a lameness when I'm riding, but I'm no expert."

"Yeah, no experts here," Cathy said. "It's on you."

"Well, in that case, Dale's in trouble," I said with a laugh. "Let's watch him walk, anyway. Between the four of us, we ought to be able to tell if his leg is going to fall off."

Cathy walked Dale down the aisle and back. The sound of his shoes on the concrete was consistent, which made me more confident than anything else that he hadn't done anything to the shoe, which was my biggest concern. I didn't want to pull the shoe off if it wasn't necessary, but I didn't want to leave it on if it wasn't right, either. That was the one part of this whole event that I wasn't 100% sure about.

A loose shoe could cause a lot of damage to his foot, and I didn't want that to happen.

"Well, I can't find anything wrong with him," I said. "How about you all?"

Emerson shrugged. "He looks good to me. Ophie?"

"Yeah, I don't think he's limping or anything."

"Okay," I said. "If anything happens to him, we'll blame the afternoon feeding crew, and Kim can yell at them when she gets back."

"Hey, we're the afternoon feeding crew," Cathy said.

I laughed. "Well, we'll think of something else, then. Let's get him in his stall so he can relax and eat breakfast." I rinsed the dirt off my tools as they put Dale away, and we met at the front door of the barn.

"Is everything else going okay?" I asked.

The girls glanced at each other. "Do you know how to fix a blower?" Ophie asked. She pointed to a cordless leaf blower by the wall. "It won't come on, it just clicks and hums."

"Holy cow, you got the horse stuck in the fence *and* you killed the blower?" I said in mock horror. "Kim is going to lose her mind!"

"I didn't kill it, it just died!" Ophie protested. "Emerson probably killed it."

"Me?" Emerson said. "I didn't even use it this whole time!"

I picked up the blower and flicked the power button. It tried to come on, but didn't quite make it. I glanced in the back end and saw that the fan blades were up against the wall of the housing on one side. Shaking it lightly didn't budge it.

"I think it's for-real dead," I said, putting it back down. "If you all leave town now, I think you can be far enough away to survive by the time Kim comes home."

"We should go to Europe," Cathy said. "We can hide in Paris and eat good cheese."

"Now that's a plan," Emerson said.

"Okay, I'm going home so I can get back to writing," I said.

"Thank you, Justin!"

"Yeah, thanks for saving the day!"

"Wait, is this going to be in a book?" Cathy asked. "Does it count as an adventure?"

I grinned. "Well, I don't know how it was for you, but it was an adventure for me! It was my first solo emergency, so it's definitely going in the book."

"Yes!" A series of high fives followed.

"Are you going to use our real names?" Emerson asked.

"No, I can't," I said, doing my best to keep a straight face. "But I was thinking about using Myrtle, Gertrude, and Ethel. What do you think?"

Cathy glanced at the others and looked at me doubtfully. "Can we pick our own names?"

I burst out laughing. "Well, if you prefer something a little more modern, I guess I could let you pick your own. Any ideas?"

It took longer to pick names than it did to get Dale out of the fence, but by the time I left, everyone was satisfied with their choice. I thought about things on the short drive home, and how different this day had been for the girls than it was for me. They were in the middle of a summer filled with horse camp, barn chores, friendship, new responsibilities, and the freedom of driving themselves around for the first time. They were making memories that would last a lifetime, and now they would even be the stars of a chapter in a book that they could keep forever.

For me, I was basking in the satisfaction of successfully dealing with a situation on my own, a position I never thought I'd be in. In every one of the hundreds of horse emergencies I'd been to, Erica was always there to make the decisions and take on the responsibility. I was proud of myself for handling this one, even if it was minor, and I knew that my confidence had increased as a result of the experience. I was also relieved that it hadn't been a disaster. If it had been, I could have called Dr. Hanks in, but that would have been worse for the horse, for the girls, and for Kim, who was out of town and helpless to intervene or manage things. That thought reminded me that I hadn't reported the outcome to Kim. I stopped on the driveway and sent her a quick text.

Rescue complete. Did not have to pull the shoe. I think he's okay. There's a decent hole in your fence, though.

Thank you!!! I'll get that fixed when I get home.

Oh, and your blower is dead, unrelated to Dale's incident.

LOL It never ends.

And it doesn't ever end. Wherever there are horses, there is something crazy, bizarre, tragic, funny, scary, silly, life-altering, stressful, or entertaining just waiting to happen. Sometimes they are good, and sometimes they are bad, but they are never boring. When you have horses, a day where nothing happens is a seldom-realized dream. But then again, when you have horses, a day where nothing happens just makes it twice as likely that tomorrow will be an absolute disaster in some way or another, so a minor event every day isn't so bad by comparison. Horses are horses, and we love them. Most of the time.

19

Final Thoughts

The world is changing, and for horses and their owners, it's now in crisis mode. Every year, the number of equine veterinarians who retire or change careers gets bigger, and the number of equine veterinarians graduating vet school and entering the work force gets smaller. To put some numbers to it, in 2020, around one hundred veterinarians left equine medicine, and four entered. There are only about two thousand equine vets in the United States, so those numbers are alarming.

Equine medicine is a difficult space to work in for a variety of reasons, both for the doctors and for the support staff. Horses are far more prone to emergencies than dogs and cats, so after-hours on-call can really become a brutal aspect of the job for a vet if they are a solo practitioner with no one to share those responsibilities with. When you have to be available 24/7 for years on end, you become consumed by it, and a lot of equine veterinarians burn out and decide to find a different line of work after a while.

Horses are unique in their ability to bring out the best and the worst in people. I do a lot of counseling with our team at the vet clinic on not taking it personally when clients call and scream at them, which happens on a regular basis. A lot of people just don't have the emotional bandwidth to see their horse in any kind of pain or discomfort, and they don't understand why the veterinarian can't get there in the next five minutes, so they rant and rave at the receptionist, or the doctor, or whoever answers the phone.

On the other end of that spectrum, grateful clients bring food into the office for the team all the time. It's almost never the same people that were losing their minds on the phone a few days prior. But I think that's a pretty fair representation of people as a whole. Some of us are so wrapped up in our own experience that we don't realize how we impact those around us. I spent the first thirty-five years of my life in that space, so I can't throw stones.

I tell you all of this because it's important that people have a realistic understanding of what's happening in the horse world, and how they are a part of things. Every horse owner needs a veterinarian. If you already have a veterinarian, it's imperative that you keep a good relationship with them. That means using them for all your routine care like vaccines and dentals every year and treating them and their staff with decency and respect. And if you don't have a vet, you need to get one, and you need to build a great relationship with them right away. Here's why:

As I mentioned, the number of equine vets is getting smaller and smaller every year. At the same time, the number of horses and horse owners is getting bigger every year. Every time a veterinarian leaves the industry, whether by retirement or career change, all the horses they were caring for have to be picked up by another veterinarian. Except that in a lot of places, there isn't another vet, or the ones that are there are swamped.

Many equine vets won't see an emergency for someone who isn't already a client, because they're just maxed out on what they can do. So, if you don't already have a vet, and you have an emergency with your horse, there might not be anyone like Erica who can come save the day. It sounds crazy, but it happens every day, and it gets worse every year. Imagine what it would be like if you called 911, and there was no ambulance to come get you. That's what's happening for horses.

So, here's something to think about. The world needs more equine veterinarians. If you're young and thinking you might be interested in this as a career, there is no shortage of jobs as an equine vet! You can go anywhere and have plenty of work to keep you busy, whether you open your own practice, or work at an existing clinic or hospital. As you've learned by now, it's hard work, and sometimes it's painful, but it's also fulfilling and rewarding in ways that can't be explained.

And if you're a parent, or a grandparent, or a friend of a young person who wants to become a veterinarian, support them. That's the most important thing you can do to ensure the future of horse health. Give kids the emotional, financial, and practical support they need to become a veterinarian. It's a very difficult path to get into vet school, and they need your help. Don't crush their dreams, help them fulfil them.

Erica and I wrote a book called *How to Become an Equine Veterinarian: A Guide for Teens.* It talks about all the things you need to do throughout high school and college to have a chance at getting into vet school. It makes a great gift for anyone over the age of 10, because it gives them a list of actionable steps they can take to start getting the experience they will need. If you don't have any kids or grandkids who are interested in that, but you still want to help, get a few copies of the book from Amazon and donate them to your local high school library or Ag class.

Here are a few things you can do to help horses and the future of vet medicine:

1. Donate money to vet school scholarships

2. Donate money to horse rescues for vet care

3. Buy books for young people, or donate them to schools

4. Donate money to your local veterinarian's emergency fund

5. Drive a young person to a vet clinic so they can shadow a doctor and get experience

6. Financially support a young person while they're in college or vet school to reduce their student loan burden

7. Buy lunch for your local vet clinic and show them you appreciate them

8. Open an account at your local feed store and buy feed and hay for someone who can't afford to feed their horses properly

Erica has committed her life to making the world a better place for horses. Since you've made it to the end of Book 3 in this series, I know that horses are important to you, too, and I want you to know that I appreciate you for sharing my journey. I try to make it both entertaining and educational, and sometimes that gets heavy, but that's the reality of horses. Sometimes it's amazing, and sometimes it's horrible, but it's all part of the big picture.

I do want to take a minute and invite you to be a part of all the things we have going on. I've made reference to a lot of stuff throughout the stories, but here is a list for you:

Vet Clinic Website: SpringhillEquine.com

Justin's Author Website: JBoydLong.com

Vet Clinic Facebook Page: Facebook.com/SpringhillEquine

YouTube Channel: YouTube.com/SpringhillEquineVet

Justin's Instagram: @JBoydLong

Justin's Facebook: Facebook.com/JBoydLong

Podcast: Straight from the Horse Doctor's Mouth
(details on our website)

Books:

Adventures of the Horse Doctor's Husband

More Adventures of the Horse Doctor's Husband

Adventures of the Horse Doctor's Husband 3

How To Become an Equine Veterinarian
(co-authored with Erica Lacher, DVM)

The Righteous Rage of a Ten-Year-Old Boy: A Journey of Self-Discovery

A great way to let people know what you think of these books is to leave a review on whatever online store you purchased them from. That's also a great way to let me know if you love it or hate it, and if I should write another one! I enjoy getting feedback from readers, and you can do that with a review, or through Instagram or Facebook. You'll see that I don't post much on social media, but I do monitor it for messages.

That's it! Thank you again for your support, and for doing your part to make the world a better place for horses. Until next time,

—Justin

Justin B. Long is a self-embracing nerd who loves crunching numbers, researching interesting things, and listening to podcasts, in addition to reading loads of books. By day he is the Hospital Administrator of Springhill Equine Veterinary Clinic, and by night he is an author, podcast host, emergency technician, and horse show husband. When he's not responding to after-hours horse emergencies or dreaming up alternate dimensions of reality, he enjoys hiking in national parks. He lives near Gainesville, Florida on a small farm with his incredible wife, 4 horses, 3 cats, 2 donkeys, 2 sheep, 2 dogs, and a lot of animal hair.